# CONTENTS

*For all the saints who from their travels rest; and especially in blessed memory of two of them, Willie Marshall and Bernard Fergusson. Also for my fellow-traveller, the lady who rode the friendly camel on the Mount of Olives.*

Best wishes
Bob Kernohan

# THE ROAD TO ZION

Travellers to Palestine and the Land of Israel

R. D. Kernohan

The Handsel Press Ltd
Edinburgh

William B. Eerdmans Publishing Company
Grand Rapids, Michigan

© Handsel Press 1995

Published jointly 1995 by
The Handsel Press Ltd
The Stables, Carberry, EH21 8PY, Scotland,
and in the United States by
Wm. B. Eerdmans Publishing Co.
255 Jefferson Ave. S.E., Grand Rapids, Michigan 49503


**British Library Cataloguing in Publication Data**

A catalogue record for this publication
is available from the British Library

ISBN 1 871828 33 3



**Library of Congress Cataloging-in-Publication Data**

Kernohan, R. D.
The road to Zion: travellers to Palestine and the land of Israel /
R. D. Kernohan.
p.        cm.
Includes bibliographical references and index.
ISBN 0-8028-0889-1
1. Christian pilgrims and pilgrimages — Palestine — History.
2. Christian pilgrims and pilgrimages — Israel — History.
3. Palestine — Description and travel.  4. Israel — Description and travel.
I. Title.
DS107.K385    1994
956.94 — dc20                                   94-40087
                                                CIP



Typeset in 11 point Garamond at the Stables, Carberry

Printed in the United States of America

# AUTHOR'S PREFACE

This book has been a labour of rather intermittent love over nearly 10 years. I hope it proves acceptable to readers, but even more that it is acceptable to God, who chose the Holy Land for things "almost too wonderful to be" and for special relationships. It is for all those who renew the encounter with the Holy Land of Palestine, which today includes the land and State of Israel, either by visiting it or by thinking about it.

It is an account of encounters with the Holy Land rather than of the land itself and its problems ancient and modern, though it cannot altogether avoid them. In the last chapters it addresses some of them, especially those affecting Christian attitudes to Israel and the Arab Palestinians. I wanted to use the past to give us better perspectives on the present state of the Holy Land, but I also want to revive interest in much that has been unfairly obscured. I believe the history of the Western Christian encounter with Palestine, especially in the nineteenth century, has been inadequately studied and undeservedly forgotten, not least in Protestant Christendom.

The book reflects the vivid impressions made on me by records of visits to the Holy Land, as well as by my own visits there, but it does not claim special expertise. I hope, however, that it may draw attention to some neglected aspects of the history of Palestine and the land of Israel, as well as to people who passed that way, a few famous and many forgotten. They are important historical witnesses. These saints who from their travels rest have much to say to those who succeed them in their pilgrimage.

Most of those who inspired the book are travellers and pilgrims who are mentioned and quoted in it. I know them only by their works, which still speak long after their death, and I have learned to love some of them and bear with the others. Some of the travels it recounts were not at all enjoyable at the time, but the experience was so intense that it deserves to be shared. Almost all of these Christians had a faith far stronger than mine, but they have helped to keep me in the faith and teach me more of its depth and breadth.

I am grateful to them, and in a more personal sense to some others, including several now dead whom I remember with affection and thanksgiving. Among them are Bernard Fergusson (Lord

v

Ballantrae) and William Marshall, from both of whom I learned much about the land and Scottish associations with it, and James Currie, in whom I saw a great power to lead others in pilgrimage. Others who helped and whom I remember with affection, loved long since and lost awhile, include Isobel Goodwin, Tom Kiltie, Lord Balerno, and James Bulloch. I also wish to record thanks to others, among them Rizek Abusharr, Samuel Hosain, Dan Ben-Dor, Iain Maciver, James Martin, Frances Macnab, Douglas Law, Professor Robert Craig, Dr John Carson, Janet Adam Smith, Frederick and Mary Levison, Canon D.M. Main, Professor Alec Cheyne, and Professor Tom Torrance, that great father of the Church in Scotland and elsewhere and great friend to the Eastern Churches and the Jewish people. I have a special debt to Jock Stein and the Handsel Press for allowing this love for my theme to be consummated.

In so far as the book contains opinions, I stand by them and accept that others may not share them. But I apologise for whatever errors it contains. Many have been corrected in draft but others will have slipped through. I retain enough of my grounding in the study of history to be well aware of the pitfalls of a subject which involves more than one academic discipline, deals with several nations and empires, and covers so many historical eras. However the subject is of very great importance and none of its many aspects should be seen in isolation.

I also apologise to those scholars and experts who may find errors and inconsistencies in my rendering of names of places and people connected with the Holy Land. I have generally had to use the forms of names adopted by those I was writing about, and in my own narrative and comments have usually opted for the forms most familiar to English-speaking people. There is no political significance in my opting to use an Arabic name or a Hebrew one.

I am grateful to several copyright holders and in one or two cases have been unable to establish whether copyright is still held and if so by whom. I apologise if I have inadvertently omitted any acknowledgement due. In particular I wish to thank the heirs of the late Sir George Adam Smith and the Trustees of the National Library of Scotland for permission to quote from his private papers and the Editor of *Life and Work* for permission to quote at length from various contributions to that journal.

*Edinburgh, February 1994*                    R.D. KERNOHAN

vi

# PART ONE: THE DIFFICULT JOURNEY

## 1  THE DESIRE AND THE DREAM

*....THAT THUMP AND LIFT OF THE HEART*

Jerusalem is a city of stone, honey-brown in the sunlight or sometimes greyish with a tinge of pink. We also think of it as the heavenly city. Zion, most prominent of four hills on which the old walled city is set, is one of the rocky outcrops of Judea, and also a state of mind and soul. It is hard to separate their history of human experience from the heavenly metaphor. For this, so millions of people believe, is a focal point of divinity's encounters with humanity.

We sing William Blake's great poetic prayer with images of Jerusalem built in England's green and pleasant land and contrasting with dark, satanic mills. In Scotland our Kirk's General Assembly disperses after singing a great metrical version of the psalm that prays for the peace of Jerusalem. In doing so we are are also seeking the "peace and felicity" of Christ's household of faith. We associate the sublimities of Handel with great tidings to Zion, and of Bach with a watchman's cry in the heavenly city. John Newton's hymn reminds us of "glorious things" spoken of it, and civic rights conferred through grace.

That city set on the hills among the Judean mountains is sacred to three religions, though in different ways. To the Jews, and therefore to Christians who believe that the New Testament is the fulfilment of promises to Israel, it is the site of the Temple, symbol and expression of the covenant between God and his people. To Muslims, the present occupants of the Temple Mount or "noble sanctuary", the Dome of the Rock there marks not only the site of of Abraham's offer to

sacrifice his son Isaac but of the Prophet Mohammed's translation to Heaven. The city's Arabic name of *El Kuds* indicates
it as a holy place.

Christians think of Jerusalem as the city (just along the
road from Bethlehem) of Calvary, Gethsemane, and the upper
room set for the Last Supper. Just outside its walls rises the
Mount of Olives, associated not only with Christ's Ascension
but with his teaching and some of his most personal expres-
sions of emotion. Its environs too are rich not just in biblical
associations but in metaphors of spiritual experience. If, like
the traveller who fell among thieves but was helped by the
Good Samaritan, we take the road down to Jericho, we might
carry on and tread the verge of Jordan. And though we may
not be sure exactly where Emmaus is, we know from Luke
that it is a seven-mile walk from Jerusalem.

Jerusalem is a city set in a territory which is both the Holy
Land and a much disputed country, now and at many times in
its history. It is also a small country. Palestine, as defined in its
boundaries by the British Mandate which preceded the restoration of the State of Israel and its conflicts with the Arabs, is
less than half the size of Scotland but rather bigger than
Vermont. But it is a small country of contrasts, as well as of
different traditions and peoples.

The land, as well as its holiest city, has a distinctive interest
for people of all three religions. For many Muslims it has
recently acquired (in addition to its Old Testament significance) a role as the symbol of political and military frustra-
tions in their dealings with the West, which is seen as the
sponsor and protector of Israel. For the Jews it is the land they
were given, where their nationality developed, for which they
longed by the waters of Babylon, and from which they were
all but totally dispersed until the modern return and restoration.

For Christians it is not only the land of Christ's birth,
crucifixion, and resurrection but of his teaching and ministry,
much of it carried on in Galilee, sometimes extending beyond
modern Palestinian or Israeli frontiers into parts of what are
now Lebanon and Syria. This is where Jesus called fishermen
from their nets to make them "fishers of men"; where he
stilled the storm and preached the Sermon on the Mount.

Palestine is also the land where the Christian Church emerged and had its first internal arguments before it spread to Macedonia, Greece, and Rome; where Saul (the Apostle Paul) "was consenting" to the murder of Stephen and set out on the memorable road to Damascus. It is also a country in which the Christian faith and the Church have had a continuous presence, in varying forms, from Pentecost till the present day.

It isn't surprising that Christians have always shown a special interest in the Holy Land, even that at times they may have confused devotion to places associated with Jesus with their commitment to follow him. At its best Christian pilgrimage of all kinds has remembered that Jesus sent his followers out to all nations and promised that where two or three people are gathered in his name - whether in Jerusalem or the ends of the earth - he is in the midst of them. Grace comes from God's forgiving love and Christ's sacrifice, not from futile bids to gain merit in God's sight.

This book is mainly about pilgrims who appreciated that, but whose motives in making the journey to Palestine - a long journey, until very recently, and at many times a hazardous one - were honourably varied. It has never really been possible to draw an absolutely firm distinction between pilgrimage and tourism, or between religious devotion and secular curiosity in seeking to fulfil what a Victorian Scotsman, Andrew Thomson, called "the desire and dream of a lifetime". Some very pious travellers had their share of human love of adventure and fascination with the strange or unknown. Other lovers of adventure - especially during the centuries of the Crusades - mixed Christian devotion in varying degrees with power-politics and even mercenary motives, sometimes also with a cruelty and intolerance of which later Christians must feel ashamed.

Many Western Christians also went to Palestine with a strong sense of duty, some to serve pilgrims and others to help and support local Christians, of whom there have always been some from the first days of the Church onwards. One particular sense of duty, especially marked among English-speaking Protestant Christians from about 1830, has been towards the Jewish people. Small communities of the Jews probably maintained a continuous, if often ignored and despised, pres-

ence in the Land from the failure of the great revolt against
Rome to the beginning of organised settlement in the last
phase of the Turkish Empire. But all Jews had a special
relationship with the Land and especially with Jerusalem.
They did not forget the city of the Temple; and they longed
for "next year in Jerusalem". Christians concerned with God's
destiny for his ancient people recognised long before the days
of political Zionism that Jerusalem - to quote the Scots
missionaries of 1839, Bonar and McCheyne - was "the centre
of the Jewish world".

In this book I write mainly of the century or thereabouts
between the Bonar-McCheyne visit, which roughly coincided
with the establishment of the Anglican diocese of Jerusalem
under a Jewish bishop, and the emergence of the State of Israel
when Britain gave up the thankless Mandate. But that story of
the road to Zion, as taken by pilgrims, missionaries, enthusiasts, and a few eccentrics, can neither be ended nor begun
abruptly.

In many ways it is an unfinished story, and therefore its
interim conclusion must take account of what has happened
since 1948. But it is also a continuous story, despite many
oscillations and diversions, from the early centuries of Christianity - even the earliest centuries of Christianity in the
British Isles. Neither the failure of the Crusades, nor the long
conflict between the Ottoman Empire and the neighbouring
Christian Powers, nor the division of the Western Church in
the age of Reformation and Counter-Reformation, entirely
cut the links between the Middle East and the Far West of
Europe.

The earliest significant and recorded British visitor to the
Holy Land is best remembered for giving his name to a heresy.
He was Pelagius, a Romanised Briton and contemporary of
another Briton, Saint Ninian, who brought Christianity to
Scotland. Pelagius was accused of abandoning the idea of
original sin and suggesting that man could earn salvation by
his own efforts. He defended his views before a synod in
Jerusalem around 415. This was about 90 years after the most
spectacular pilgrimage visit of the early Christian era, when
the Empress Helena allegedy found not only the site of the
holy sepulchre but the remains of "the true cross". Helena was

the mother of Constantine, who made Christianity the recognised religion of the Roman Empire and moved the imperial capital to Byzantium - better known since as Constantinople.

But the father of British travel-writing about the Holy Land is Adamnan, ninth Abbot of Iona, biographer of Saint Columba, and editing ghost-writer and publisher of *De Locis Sanctis*, an early eighth-century account of visits to various holy places about 700 by Arculf, a bishop in Gaul. Adamnan's book, publicised by Bede, "father of English history", is a mixture of pious fancy and valuable reporting. For example he dwells on a theme that was to recur in most travel-writing about Jerusalem until the late nineteenth-century: the stink of the Old City, with its six gates and 84 towers. But he saw a special providence of God in the timing of the rains that came after the city's great commercial fair in September to clear the steets of a vast quantity of dung left by camels, horses, mules, and oxen - and in the topography that washed it all into the Brook Kidron and the Valley of Jehoshaphat. "A heavy fall of rain begins on the night following and ceases only when the city has been perfectly cleansed."

Arculf also testifies to the extent to which various cults of relics had become established, as well as to the credulity of the times. He kissed "the cup of our Lord, of the capacity of about a French quart". He believed he saw the sponge that was held up to the man on the cross and the lance which pierced Jesus' side. In the middle of the city he noted a pillar which cast no shadow at noon on the summer solstice, "which shows that this is the centre of the earth".

A generation later an unknown nun serving as a missionary in Germany was the first British woman travel-writer about the Holy Land. She wrote up the account by her kinsman Willibald, probably a Hampshire man who became a bishop in Germany, of his visit to "the square house cut in rock", as he called the cave under the Church of the Nativity in Bethlehem, built by the Emperor Constantine in 330 on the supposed and quite possible site of Christ's birth. Willibald also bathed in the Jordan, drank from a wine-vessel at Cana of Galilee, and noted that there was a Jewish synagogue at Tiberias.

Already a handful of pilgrims from the Far West of Christendom were making the long and dangerous journey to Palestine, despite the risks of war, fever, shipwreck, and the hazardous landing at Jaffa. This choppy landfall is another recurring theme of pilgrimage literature until quite recently, for the Holy Land had no good port after the decay of Caesarea until the development of Haifa in the twentieth century. For example the early twelfth-century English pilgrim and merchant Saewulf, whom the historian William of Malmesbury describes as alternating between episodes of sin and penitence, dwells on the "sudden great desire of landing" which made him risk the first chance to get on shore. Before his hired boat reached the shore, "the sea was troubled and became continually more tempestuous". The most graphic part of his narrative is the description of the havoc wrought on a fleet of 30 ships, "all laden with palmers and with merchandise". The violence of the wind would not allow them to put out to sea "and the character of the coast would not allow them to put into shore with safety". Only a handful of those who were shipwrecked, he reported, reached the shore alive.

But even on shore there were many dangers, and the rocky road up to Jerusalem was marked by what the wild beasts had left of pilgrim corpses. Their comrades had no time to bury stragglers but hurried on, fearful of marauding Saracens - though even more victims, said Saewulf, were cut off by heat and thirst or by drinking too much.

Saewulf was writing in the first phase of the series of wars history calls the Crusades, a few years after the capture of the Holy City, the infamous massacre of Jews and Muslims there, and the creation of the "Latin" Kingdom of Jerusalem. This was Western Christendom's attempt not only to overthrow the Muslim rule which in various forms had already dominated Syria and Palestine for several centuries but to overawe the Eastern Church. After the Arab conquest of the seventh century Islam came to displace Christianity as the predominant religion, and the Dome of the Rock and the Aksa Mosque were built on the Temple Mount in Jerusalem. These political complications - like many that were to follow - compounded the already considerable difficulties facing the pilgrim but they never destroyed the Christian presence in Palestine.

Neither did they interrupt for any prolonged period the flow of Christian visitors, though many of them in the Crusading era were writing military memoirs rather than testaments of devotion.

This was neither the first nor the last era in which human motives were mixed, and those who like to explore paradoxes and complexities of history will find plenty to interest them in the mingled piety and power-politics of the Crusading era. The story is too complicated even to attempt to summarise here, but two important points are worth making.

The first is that the Crusades are best seen not merely as a confrontation of Christian and Muslim Arab (or Saracen) in Palestine. Much of the conflict was nowhere near Jerusalem and little concerned with its fate. The Crusades were phases in a conflict of cultures and civilisations which extended much more widely in the Middle East and the Mediterranean, even as far West as Spain and Portugal. The fervently crusading French king later known as Saint Louis died attacking Tunis. And as Scots schoolchildren ought to know, Sir James Douglas set out to take King Robert Bruce's heart to the Holy Land but died - hurling the casket into the battle - in a stramash with the Moors in Spain. However there were many cross-currents in the conflict and many people, especially Eastern Christians, who did not fit neatly into the two main camps.

The second is that the Crusades have long bred historical myths - sometimes given literary form as by Torquato Tasso in sixteenth-century Italy and Sir Walter Scott in nineteenth-century Scotland. But the myths are not on one side only, and may be more significant today on the Arab side. Even in 1917, when General Allenby captured Jerusalem from the Turks, the matter was sensitive enough to induce unsuccesful attempts to deter journalists and the troops themselves from talking in terms of a belated "crusading" victory. Since then the various Arab conflicts with the West and the Jewish-Arab quarrel over Palestine have bred a curious hybrid of romantic and revolutionary enthusiasms. The conflicts of the Middle Ages and the Crusaders' eventual defeat are presented in terms of twentieth-century anti-imperialism, and in particular the "intrusion" of the modern Israel into the Middle East is related to the fate of the Crusader States, notably the Kingdom of

Jerusalem, which established a presence on the Eastern Mediterranean shore but were finally driven into the sea.

There is another Western myth which is based on a major misconception: the idea of a monolithic Islam. Although Jerusalem was under Muslim rule from 637 to 1917, Islamic domination was expressed in very different ways and by very varied ruling castes or imperialisms. Early caliphs were fairly tolerant of Christians and their holy places; yet one in the eleventh century sent in demolition squads to smash up the Church of the Holy Sepulchre. Some rulers came from Egypt or elsewhere in the Arab world, others from Asia Minor. Before the long ascendancy and gradual decay of the Ottoman Turkish Empire there had been an earlier phase of Seljuk Turkish rule.

During several centuries when Palestine seemed politically no more than a backward and outlying part of Syria, Arabic in language and culture and mainly Muslim in religion, the whole Middle East was under the domination not of Arabs but of Turks. It is an irony of history that the Arab nationalism which protested, and still protests, about Jewish settlement in Palestine took shape even later than political Zionism, and that in its early years this movement, which the West associates with Islam, was disproportionately influenced by the Christian Arab minority.

Despite these many political changes, sometimes accompanied by religious intolerance, a tradition of Christian pilgrimage to the Holy Land continued unbroken. In the later Middle Ages the memory of the Crusades did not prevent the growth of a substantial pilgrimage-tourist industry organised from Venice. Chaucer expected his readers to find it credible, as well as mildly amusing, that the Wife of Bath had made three trips to Jerusalem.

Although a return passage could be had for 50 or 60 ducats, there were inclusive prices for package tours by large galleys - Venice back to Venice, with guides, lodging, and "the holy circuit" included. These were much more expensive but better value. There were also formal contracts, stipulations of what was included not unlike those at the back of today's brochures, and guidance on how to minimise the risk of pillage by the Saracens, over and above the Government taxes on

Christian and Jewish pilgrims which were a major source of local revenue. Comparisons with modern prices are almost impossible but the Venetian galleys seem to have offered better value than anything up to the coming of Cook's tours. The cost is said to have doubled when the wars with the Turks brought the end of the regular galley service.

With the contract came guidance. Some of it reflects the subservience demanded of Christians under Muslim rule and some testifies to the follies of human nature, then and now. Don't ever return a blow from a Saracen. Don't gaze at the local women, for husbands are hyper-jealous. Don't on any account respond when a woman beckons the pilgrim to enter a house, for he's liable to be robbed and even murdered by men in league with her. "Those who aren't careful about such things run into great danger."

There is also evidence that armchair travellers were catered for. There was a medieval best-seller of Eastern Mediterranean and Holy Land travel published in England, in Latin and French as well as English, and attributed to Sir John Maundeville. It included an account of a visit to the Temple Mount and its mosques, then and for long afterwards barred to Christians. Some modern scholars doubt whether Maundeville, said to have been born in St Albans, ever existed. If he didn't, it was still commercially profitable to invent him and attribute to him bits and pieces of other travellers' tales. Long afterwards Shakespeare's audiences still found it appropriate that he should use the story that King Henry 1V of England, having vainly supposed a prophecy meant he would die in the Holy Land, made a good end in the Jerusalem Chamber at Westminster.

The Jerusalem connection and the tradition of Holy Land travel also survived the addition of a new division within Western Christendom to the old one between the Roman and Greek Churches. Protestants scorned medieval styles of pilgrimage, were sceptical of the holy places and relics associated with them, and rejected the idea that pious deeds and travels could, under the Church's jurisdiction, contribute to remission of the penalties of sin or earn salvation by some scheme of points accumulation. They did not necessarily reject the spiritual concept of pilgrimage. John Bunyan turned it into a classic both of Christian and English prose, though his pilgrim progressed through the trials of ordinary life and a landscape of seventeenth-century England.

But Protestants who found no theological reasons for pilgrimage could still be intensely interested and curious about the Holy Land, both intellectually and spiritually, even though they had to cross countries where they were suspect as heretics before reaching those where they were scorned and taxed as infidels.

They were relatively few, and they lacked both the opportunities and fervour - especially fervour for Jewish missions - which makes it epigrammatically possible to think of the early nineteenth century as the time of "the Protestant discovery of Palestine". But those few are worth remembering, for what they were and the new light in which they surveyed what they found. For example the great chronicler of English voyages, Richard Hakluyt, records the voyage of an English merchant-pilgrim, Laurence Aldersey, in 1581. He had some trouble on the voyage between Venice and Cyprus when he declined to sing either *Ave Maria* or *Salve Regina* and to kiss the image of the Virgin. Once on shore in Palestine his main troubles were with the "Arabians" and he complained that a series of petty extortions backed by threats cost 20 shillings a head, despite the guard that had been hired. A more significant, but equally Protestant traveller was the Scotsman, William Lithgow, who made the serious mistake of travelling through the Spanish realms of the Inquisition. He suffered torture, first to discover whether he was a spy and then to convince him that the Pope was the Vicar of Christ. But in the course of his 20 years' travelling he reached Palestine in 1612, had the pilgrim's Jerusalem cross tattooed on his skin, and discomfited the father-guardian of the Latin monastery in Jerusalem after the ritual feet-washing, for this pilgrim's privilege was not supposed to be extended to Protestants. Lithgow returned to Scotland bringing a pound of "white Bethlehem earth" as a present for James VI's queen, Anne of Denmark. He was understandably sceptical about the claim that it came from the spot where Mary's milk had spilt upon the ground. Lithgow is also credited with having visited more places in Europe than any other traveller of his time.

Other English-speaking visitors to the Holy Land included the notable travellers George Sandys, who like his contemporary Lithgow left details of exactions and extortions by the
Turks, and Fynes Moryson, who summed up his post-Refor-
mation motives for going to Jerusalem in 1596: "I had no
thought to expiate the least sin of mine. Much less did I hope
to merit any grace from God. But when once I had begun to
visit foreign parts I was so stirred up by emulation and
curiosity as I never did behold any without a kind of sweet
envy who in this kind had dared more than myself."

That could also have been the epitaph for the Somerset
parson's son and friend of Ben Jonson, Thomas Coryate, a
compulsive traveller who left his bones in India in 1617 but
wrote the most notable of early travel books in English, the
*Crudities*. He has been credited with the introduction of the
fork into British table manners but he was another kind of
pioneer. On his way to the Holy Land he had to be rescued
from the Venice ghetto after an attempt to convert the Jews
there. He also left a record of the souvenir trade in Jerusalem
which shows that bad taste is no modern monopoly and that
the early seventeenth century had its equivalent of the hideous
T-shirts on sale today in the Old City. In 1615 popular lines
included garters and girdles inscribed in gold *Santo Sepulchro*.

The Protestants from the West were probably a small
minority of a diminished number of pilgrims. It is even
possible that around 1600 there were more Jewish pilgrims to
the Holy Land that Western Christian ones. The flow was
reduced not only by Western Christendom's divisions and its
new interest in a New World but by the hazards of the country
and the far-ranging conflict with the Ottoman Empire, whose
armies besieged Vienna later in the seventeenth century. In
1612, for example, the Western Easter was celebrated with
only 19 "Franks" - as Western Christians were called - in
Jerusalem. In the Middle East the turmoil of the Reformation
and the ferocity of the Counter-Reformation had not altogether destroyed the cultural unity of the Franks.

For in and around the Holy Land the great divisions were
between Muslims and Christians (and between both and the
Jews). Even among the Christians the old schism of East and
West, between the Greek world and the Latin one, counted

for more than the new one among the Franks. The twentieth-century traveller will still find a new perspective on matters ecumenical in Jerusalem as he encounters Greek, Armenian, Coptic, and other Eastern traditions, for some of whom Rome still seems as much an upstart as a menace.

The Protestant-Roman Catholic relationship was uneasy. The Franciscans (who had a special role in looking after pilgrims) were not quite sure how heartily to welcome those they deplored as heretics. The Protestants sometimes distrusted them unfairly - even suspecting poisoning when the real cause of intestinal afflictions was almost certainly the heat, dirt, and stink of a most unhygienic holy city.

Curiosity continued to break through the barriers which isolated Turkish-ruled Palestine from the West and some of those who came to the Middle East to trade remained to pray. One remarkable pilgrim who helped them was Henry Maundrell, a conscientious diarist who had been a fellow of Exeter College, Oxford before becoming chaplain to the English Levant Company's trading station or "factory" at Aleppo in Northern Syria. In 1697 Maundrell, a founding father of the minister-led group tour, took a party of 14 of the company's staff across Syria into Palestine, where he made geological and other scientific observations. He noted that the Jordan valley seemed impregnated with salt even at some distance from the Dead Sea and touched on a theme that was to become very evident in later Protestant reflections on the state of the land. In Judea, he said, they passed among hills and valleys "all of a very barren aspect at present but discovering evident signs of the labour of the husbandman in ancient times".

Another Oxford man to add the pilgrimage to a chaplaincy in the Muslim world - this time at the factory in Algiers - was Thomas Shaw, who survived a trip in which he was "barbarously used and insulted" to become eventually principal of St Edmund Hall and the university's professor of Greek. He is an important witness to the near-anarchy which descended on parts of the Ottoman Empire and which eventually allowed or encouraged the Western Powers to intervene there, with dramatic consequences for the Holy Land. Shaw reported that between Suez and Mount Sinai and on the coast travellers could find safety in numbers. But almost all the 6000 pilgrims in his caravan on the way from Rama to Jerusalem in 1722 suffered assault or robbery, despite the presence of several escorting Turkish detachments. Whole clans of Arabs, from 50 to 500 strong, were hovering around in search of booty. He himself was twice taken hostage on the journey "for the payment of unreasonable demands", though rescued by a larger Turkish force sent out from Jerusalem.

But by the end of the eighteenth century a new world was taking shape. The Turkish Empire sank into further decline. Napoleon Bonaparte invaded Egypt, massacred prisoners at Jaffa, fought battles near Nazareth and Mount Tabor, and marched as far as Acre, where the British sea-power which destroyed his fleet at the mouth of the Nile landed sailors to stiffen the defence. He also dabbled with two notions which had significance for others even after his mind had moved to other imperial dreams. He thought of encouraging the Arabs to rebel against their Turkish rulers; and he briefly sought Jewish support with a grandiloquent proclamation to "the rightful heirs of Palestine".

There had also been religious and cultural movements in the West which focussed attention on the Holy Land in a way that had scarcely been known since the Crusades, but in a quite different spirit. The French romantic and Catholic revivalist Chateaubriand visited Palestine in 1806, claiming that Jerusalem had been almost forgotten and that "an anti-religious century had lost its memory of the cradle of religion". For a Frenchman he also had the unusual virtue of being able to quote John Milton. But two very different romantics had immense influence on the English-speaking world. Sir Walter Scott romanticised the Crusades and Byron the most effective and spectacular revolt against Ottoman power, that of the Greeks. There had also been several important Middle Eastern journeys by Western travellers who mixed scientific research with the excitement of discovery. But another movement, remote from Byron's outlook and even the placidity of Scott's Christianity, had reshaped the religious life of the English-speaking world: the Evangelical revival.

It did not merely look to Palestine as a cradle of religion or as the scene of dramatic events in medieval Christian history. It shared the interest in the country's topography, economy, geology, and ancient remains but it went further. Some, at least, of those influenced by the revival pondered Palestine's destiny rather than its past and thought of the land when they reflected and prayed about God's ancient people, the Jews, of whose return to the Promised Land, in the due time and providence of God, Milton had written in *Paradise Regained*:

> Yet he at length, time to himself best known,
> Remembering Abraham, by some wondrous call
> May bring them back repentant and sincere.

This was the age when Protestant Christianity, for the first time, faced up to the challenge of world-wide mission. William Carey sailed for India in 1793. Two years later the London Missionary Society took shape. The British and Foreign Bible Society was founded in 1804, the year of the formation of a Palestine Association for promoting exploration and research in the Holy Land. And by 1809 there was a London Society for Promoting Christianity among the Jews, later the Church Missions to Jews. Had not the Apostle Paul three times in his letter to the Christians at Rome about God's purposes emphasised the words: "To the Jew first ...?"

Even in the early nineteenth century Christian consideration of relations with the Jewish people, and of the promises offered "to the Jew first", focussed attention on Palestine. Small Jewish communities survived there and some Jews of the dispersion came as pilgrims, or to die, but there was a broader and deeper relationship between the land and its ancient people. "On whatever part of the earth's surface they have their abode, their eyes and their faith are all pointed in the same direction - to the land of their fathers and the holy city where they worshipped."

So wrote Dr Michael Russell, a clergyman explaining the history and condition of Palestine to English-speaking Christians in 1831. Long before political Zionism was thought of, but reflecting on that Napoleonic proclamation of 30 years before, he said that the Jews "in every commotion which affects Syria are accustomed to look for the indications of that happy change destined in the eyes of their faith to restore the Kingdom of Israel in the latter days."

In the West there was also intense political and diplomatic interest in the commotions of Syria, especially the possibility that a rising new power in Egypt might take over all or part of the Ottoman Empire. The military, naval, and diplomatic ascendancy of the West, the technological revolution in travel which was already under way, and the peace which Europe enjoyed after the Napoleonic wars - all these made it easier for travellers to visit the Holy Land. Some went for romantic or literary motives. Among them were the French poet Lamartine; the young Disraeli, always proud of his Jewish ancestry; Alexander Kinglake, author of the immensely successful *Eothen*; and Robert Curzon, who travelled eastward when he lost his parliamentary borough through the Great Reform Bill. Curzon was to leave a dramatic account of one special "commotion", the disaster in the Church of the Holy Sepulchre at the 1834 Greek Easter ceremony of the Holy Fire, when he narrowly escaped a mixture of panic and brutality which left hundreds of worshippers dead.

But some of the most determined travellers were the evangelical Christians, including those with a special interest in the Jews. They were watching for signs of the times, sensing that some of the most dramatic changes in the long history of the Holy Land were about to take place. A small backward Turkish territory, with a small untidy and often dirty city as a minor local capital, was to resume some of its old importance in the world, and to become the focal point for new conflicts. And a growing and signficant number of Western Christians were to visit Palestine and reflect on their faith in the land of God's promises and Jesus' ministry.

Christians have to beware of any idolatry of the land or of the places within it that history and custom have deemed "holy". But those coming to it have always felt what a wartime British visitor in uniform, John Connell, called "that thump and lift of the heart". It is a natural and recurring reaction.

# 2   THE SCOTS RECONNAISSANCE

*BONAR, MCCHEYNE, AND SIR MOSES MONTEFIORE*

Towards noon on July 9, 1839 two Frankish travellers, as the local people called them, rested by the pool and fountain in the courtyard of the caravanserai or great inn in the Lebanese biblical city of Sidon. They were young Scotsmen in their twenties on a journey from Beirut to Galilee, waiting for one of their mules to be shod but glad to rest from the heat. Even on the coast July is fiercely hot in Lebanon.

A vine had been trailed over the pool, which was surrounded by a few orange trees. So the travellers noted; they also wrote in their diary that they saw two Druse women wearing the distinctive *tantour* or "horn upon the forehead", which they suggested had a biblical origin. But they were recording what they thought as well as what they saw, reflecting especially on the city's decline.

All the magnificence of Sidon was gone, they noted, and added: "For God has executed judgments in her." The thought and the words had originally been those of the Hebrew prophet Ezekiel, but Robert Murray McCheyne and Andrew Bonar, ministers of the Church of Scotland, believed them to be both true and meaningful in 1839.

They saw only one notable modern building, a public bath. In their diary they noted that some buildings dated back to the time of the Crusaders who dominated this coast for two centuries and that the caravanserai had once been "Frankish". That was probably a mistake, for it must have been the *khan* built by a sixteenth-century sultan. Around it, they wrote, they had "frequently stumbled upon broken pillars and fragments of carved stones, the memorials of former greatness." They noted that the city seemed to have no great merchants and little trade except for necessities of life in the bazaar. Shops offered only a few fishing rods for sale.

It was placid by the pool, but presently there came a commotion. A string of camels arrived, even more heavily burdened than usual. They were laden with furniture which seemed to come from an establishment of some substance and a more European taste than was customary in the Ottoman Empire. For the camel-train was bringing down to the coast for sale the moveable property of Lady Hester Stanhope, the spectacularly eccentric Englishwoman (cousin of William Pitt and once his housekeeper at Downing Street) who for more than 25 years lived in a hill-villa among the Druse people and had only recently died there. Lady Hester was what later journalists would call a legend in her lifetime, a romantic celebrity associated in the public mind with all that seemed mysterious and even gorgeous in the East. "There is a longing for the East very commonly felt by proud-hearted people when goaded by sorrow", wrote Alexander Kinglake, who fitted a long interview with her into *Eothen*.

A very different sense of mystery, as well as the "goading" of a practical sense of duty, had taken Bonar and McCheyne to South Lebanon and Palestine - both areas at that time often reckoned as part of "Syria". In that meeting at Sidon between the clergymen and the camel-train two very different Western attitudes to the Middle East briefly encountered each other, the one fired by a secular sense of adventure and romance, mingling freethinking with mysticism; the other shaped not only by a human sense of purpose but a reverence for divine revelation and an expectation of a destiny about to be disclosed. Lady Hester dreamed of riding with a Messiah through the gates of Jerusalem. Bonar and McCheyne knew he had long since ridden into Jerusalem on an ass, a few days before his trial and execution. The two attitudes co-existed and even sometimes overlapped for the rest of the nineteenth century and have survived into our own century, despite dramatic changes in the political and social background.

For all Christians one small part of the Middle East, including Palestine and some border areas of Lebanon and Syria, has a special interest, even a kind of holiness, because Jesus spent his earthly life there. The Sidon area is recorded in the Gospels as the most northerly one which he visited in his ministry. It was somewhere there that he healed the daughter

of a Canaanite woman whose faith overcame his feeling that
he was sent only to "the lost sheep of the house of
Israel"(Matthew 15).

The house of Israel was also the primary concern of Bonar
and McCheyne, who found that Sidon had 300 Jews, about 20
or 30 of whom they met in the synagogue and two hospitable
houses. Coffee-drinking, courtesies, and controversies were
mingled in the visit. A French-speaking rabbi from Algeria
accepted a Hebrew tract and showed the visitors a venerable
manuscript of the Jewish law. An older rabbi produced a
Hebrew New Testament but argued about it. McCheyne read
part of Ezekiel 37, about the dry bones that shall live, to a
Jewish shopkeeper, and Bonar had Jewish children reading
from Matthew's Gospel in Hebrew.

Later, with the mule shod, the two Scots and their party,
which included Greek Catholic, Christian Syrian, Maronite,
and Druse servants, set off towards Tyre. They were warned
that a traveller on that road had been murdered by Arabs the
day before, but decided to trust in God. That night they
pitched their tent on grass-grown ruins in a dilapidated *khan*,
listening to jackals and wary of scorpions. So ended a fairly
ordinary day in one of the most extraordinary of Scottish
enterprises, the "Mission of Inquiry to the Jews from the
Church of Scotland". It was an expedition which also reached
Asia Minor, Constantinople, Romania, Prussian Poland, and
Central Europe, and the "Narrative" of it produced by Bonar
(who did most of the writing) and McCheyne is a classic of
both religious and travel literature, a neglected treasure both
of Scottish history and the universal Church.

It is also an important if far from infallible historical
source about the condition of the Holy Land, as seen by
Western Protestant eyes, at a fateful time in its history. And
because the Scots were so concerned with the Jews - "to see the
real conditions and character of God's ancient people" was
their one object in view, they said - it is an important
assessment of the Jewish interest in Palestine at the time.

It is independent of the hindsight and bias often involved
in historical arguments which developed after the rise both of
Zionism and Arab nationalism.

But there is no doubt that the land as well as the cause had an intense fascination for these biblical Christians. They dwelt minutely, they said, on the scenery of the Holy Land and the manners of its inhabitants "because anything that may invest that land with interest will almost necessarily lead the reader to care for the peculiar people who once possessed it and still claim it as their own." There was no doubting their own intense interest.

The Scots mission was something between a practical reconnaissance and a spiritual exploration. Formally commissioned by the Kirk's Committee for the Conversion of the Jews, the plan derived much of its driving force at home from Dr Robert Candlish, who was later to succeed Thomas Chalmers as the outstanding leader of the Free Church of Scotland which emerged from the Disruption of 1843. It was Candlish who, walking one day in 1838 with McCheyne and talking to him about the "mission to Israel", asked him to consider the long and arduous expedition, meant to settle how the Kirk might plan a Jewish mission and where it might operate.

It was a remarkable suggestion. McCheyne was only 25, yet was in effect to be the real leader of the expedition. But he was already showing the first signs of the tuberculosis that was to kill him a few years later, and had temporarily given up his work at St Peter's in Dundee. There seemed some prospect that sea-voyages and a spell in a warmer climate might help his convalescence, and doctors agreed that the "calm steady excitement" of the trip might also help. But the doctors may not have fully appreciated other hazards of the Eastern Mediterranean summer. A fortnight after the visit to Sidon, McCheyne was sorely stricken by fever in Beirut and was advised by the Christian Jewish doctor who tended him that there was less danger in the sea-voyage via Cyprus to Asia Minor than cooped up in the Lebanon. He was desperately ill on board ship with no medical aid until the landing at Smyrna, where he had to be left behind until he was well enough to catch up with Bonar at Constantinople.

There were four ministers on the trip, the only elder nominated having withdrawn on health grounds. By an irony of history McCheyne was the only one of them who was to die within the "established" Church of Scotland, for he did not live to see the Disruption. The other three - Bonar, and the two older members, Professor Black of Aberdeen and Dr Alexander Keith of St Cyrus - all "came out" and into the Free Church, which won the overwhelming support of the supporters of the Kirk's Jewish and foreign missions. Even in 1839 the news from home which the expedition awaited most anxiously and eagerly was of the gathering conflict of Church and courts in Scotland. In Jerusalem, for example, they heard the news of the House of Lords decision against the Church in the Auchertarder case, and even wondered if there was a prophetic link between this time of trial and the deliverance of Israel.

They had set out in April via Paris, braced to face "the awful profanation of the holy Sabbath" they expected there, and which they duly found. Their itinerary illustrates how the industrial revolution and the coming of steam were changing conditions of travel. In France they still had to bump along by diligence until they reached the Saône, from which a succession of river-steamboats took them to Marseilles. From there they sailed to Egypt in steamers, via Genoa, Leghorn, and Malta, finding that ships' engineers on the Mediterranean were English, Scots, or Ulster Protestants. They also encountered one of the complexities of Jewish life in the great dispersion. On the ship to Alexandria the Sephardic Jews they met, and with whom they conversed after a fashion in Hebrew and Italian, spoke a Spanish dialect among themselves. Later the Scots' gift of languages was to be even more diversely employed, for they found their Greek and Latin useful, spoke to Jews in German and French as well as Hebrew, and learned some basic Arabic.

The plan was for the Scots to find a coasting ship at Alexandria and reach either Jaffa or Beirut. They had an unpleasant surprise. There was plague in Egypt and they faced the prospect of quarantine before being allowed to sail. The outcome was that they approached the Promised Land from the same quarter as the Children of Israel and by the subsequent route of the Scottish Lowland Territorial Division in the campaign of 1917. After getting across the Nile Delta by boat they transferred to ships of the desert and took the camel-track across Sinai, then by the coastal town of El Arish. To guide and sustain them they had two Arab servants who spoke Italian, the *lingua franca* since the days of Venetian greatness for Eastern Mediterranean contacts between Franks and natives. One had also acquired English in the service of the American Professor Robinson, a pioneer scholar whose research into Palestine's antiquities and historical geography was to be frequently cited in the travellers' tales of the rest of the nineteenth century. The Scots had spent upwards of £17 on tents, equipment, and provisions and contracted to pay each servant about £12, covering the cost of three months' service and expenses for the return to Egypt.

It was hard going in unaccustomed conditions, especially for Professor Black, who fell from a camel in Sinai and felt the effects for the rest of the trip. Yet it was a voyage of delight for the Scots. Every sight, almost every step, summoned up a scriptural allusion. When the camels were made to lie down at evening it was as if they were with Abraham's servant, waiting for the women to come to the well to draw water. Camel hair made them think of John the Baptist's raiment. When they saw herds of goats mingled with sheep in their grazing they thought of Jesus' parable of the Last Judgment. When they saw distant mountains they thought of Moses' eagerness after years in the wilderness to see the good land beyond. When they were scorched by the sun they wondered if this had inspired the Psalmist when he wrote: "I am afflicted and ready to die from my youth up."

When they passed by Gaza and into the Holy Land itself the experience became even more intense, as much spiritual as intellectual. Around them biblical prophecy seemed abundantly fulfilled. Hadn't Zechariah foretold (9.5) that kings would perish from Gaza, where there was now only a "paltry governor ... helping travellers find camels for their journey"? Further on, where Zephaniah had spoken (2.6-7) of the seacoast becoming "dwellings and cottages for shepherds and folds for their flocks" they noted how few fields were cultivated. And they pondered over a strange vision of the prophet that the remnant of the house of Judah would lie down in the houses of Ashkelon "for the Lord shall visit them and turn away their captivity". Speedily may the promise come to pass, wrote Bonar in the journal. Perhaps it did, long afterwards. So it seemed to the South African Jewish company which in 1953 developed New Ashkelon and inscribed the prophecy over a gateway dedicated to Zephaniah.

As the Scottish party moved towards the hills they noted that the villages seemed relics of something much greater. As they began to climb towards Jerusalem they found overgrown and crumbled terraces and masses of briers: "We felt a secret joy in beholding the deserted terraces and the fields over-run with thorns; for when we saw the word of threatening so clearly and literally fulfilled, our unbelief was reproved, and we were taught to expect without a shadow of a doubt that the promised blessing would be as full and sure." The Holy Spirit would be poured out as a flood on Israel and both land and people would become a garden of the Lord.

There was a mystical experience in their observation of the land around them, and in their anticipation of their feet standing in Jerusalem. As they drew nearer McCheyne dismounted from his camel and ran ahead to be the first to see the Holy City. When the others caught up there was confusion as well as excitement, for in the clear air they were not sure which were the mountains of Moab beyond the Jordan and which the hills around Jerusalem.

Then as they passed at last through the Jaffa Gate into the city their thoughts turned to one of Jeremiah's lamentations (2.15): "Is this the city which men call the perfection of beauty, the joy of the whole earth?" They looked at dark walls, slippery narrow streets, a poor ill-clad population. "But we were soon to learn that all the elements of Jerusalem's glory and beauty are still remaining in its wonderful situation, fitting it to be once again in the latter day the city of the Great King."

The party reached Jerusalem on June 7, 1839, two months after leaving Scotland, and stayed there till June 18 before setting out through Samaria and by what remained of "the excellency of Carmel" to Haifa. There they made one of their few concessions to the troubled state of the Ottoman Empire in general and of Syria, Lebanon, and Palestine in particular. The empire was uneasily divided between the Sultan's main dominions and the semi-independent territories of Mehemet

Ali in Egypt and his son Ibrahim, who was governor in Palestine and Syria. In 1839 it drifted again into civil war and Ibrahim had just won a battle far to the north at Nezib, but the absence of his army had endangered what little law and order there was in the countryside.

After some persuasion by the British vice-consul, the party decided that overland travel was dangerous and negotiated a passage to Beirut in a large open boat on which they spent a chilly night at sea, trying to follow Jesus' example by seeking untroubled sleep in uncomfortable conditions. The Lebanese port, though it had only a small Jewish community, was a major centre for Western missions, educational as well as evangelical and much more than Jerusalem a meeting-place of West and East. The Americans had already established the presence from which a major university and cultural influence was to evolve. Those who welcomed the Scots there and whom they consulted included William Thomson, the American missionary-educator who later wrote the immensely successful *The Land and the Book* - and who in 1839 had recently conducted the burial service for Lady Hester Stanhope.

Beirut was also to provide the parting of the ways for the Scots party, with the two older members turning for home via Constantinople and the Danube. This decision, enforced by the state of Black's health, was to have it own significant results, for it led to the establishment of an important Scots mission in Budapest. But it also left Bonar and McCheyne to resume their travels in the Holy Land itself, reaching Galilee by that journey through South Lebanon which involved the brief halt in Sidon. Their stay in the Holy Land and Lebanon lasted until July 28, when they set off on an extraordinary homeward journey by way of the Bosphorus, Moldavia and Wallachia (the modern Romania), and Austrian Poland, frustrated in their hope of getting a Russian visa to let them visit the main centres of Polish Jewry. "Russia holds Israel", they said, "with a grip as firm as that of Pharaoh". It was well into November before they were back in Scotland.

Bonar composed the main part of the daily chronicle of the journey, with McCheyne contributing sketches and consultation. At times, perhaps, he is McCheyne's Boswell, though all the travellers shared the joy of hearing "the voice

of the turtle" in the land or the awe of remembering a
prophecy of Micah (3.12) when they came across an Arab
farmer ploughing on Mount Zion. Their book is one which
sorely needs a new edition, though Bonar's biography of his
friend, which contains some of McCheyne's letters about the
journey, is in modern print. Many modern Christians will
find its theology of election too stern and exclusive. Not all the
evidences of prophecies fulfilled are convincing, for sometimes the travellers saw what they wished to see. Nor are all
its assessments of the situation in the Holy Land as authoritative as this book of intense and persuasive conviction makes
them sound, for Bonar and McCheyne were authorities
neither on the Muslim Middle East's history and culture nor
on the Eastern Question in the politics and diplomacy of their
own day.

Modern Orthodox Jews will disagree with them, as did the
rabbis they engaged in argument after joining in worship at
the synagogues, about the fulfilment of the Old Testament.
Secularised Jews will be immune to lines of argument that rely
so heavily and literally on Scripture. Yet Jews as well as
Christians should rediscover them - not least because they
demand reappraisal of much that is assumed about Jewish
missions and "religious anti-semitism". Far from being anti-
semitic they were (like many Anglican enthusiasts for the
same cause) passionately pro-Jewish - so much so that one
suspects they wearied a great many of their more apathetic
fellow-Christians who were touched by the relatively mild
British anti-Jewish prejudices of the time. Although their aim
was the conversion of the Hebrew people into a Christian
nation, their work belongs not only to an episode in mission
but to the longer story of Christian-Jewish relations.

To that they contributed much, including a shared love of
the land of an intensity no modern Zionist could surpass.
They also recorded some useful and friendly encounters,
notably with Sir Moses Montefiore, and a great deal of
historically valuable and objective information about the
condition of the Jews they met, including those then in
Palestine. Anyone who reads their account, and between its
lines, will also come across attitudes and information which

have their value in the history of Christianity too, and not least of evangelical ecumenism.

Sir Moses Montefiore is one of the great figures of modern Jewish history. Born in Leghorn, he came to London, made a fortune on the Stock Exchange, was president of the Sephardic Jewish community, and campaigned for the removal of civil disabilities which restricted the role of Jews in British public life. He became enough of an "establishment" figure to be high sheriff of Kent and a sheriff of London and was also the grand old man of world Jewry when he died in 1885 aged 101. His most lasting achievement was as a philanthrophist-prophet, improving the condition of the Jewish people in various countries (for there were far more very poor Jews than rich Jews) and giving purpose and direction to their longing for a presence in the Holy Land. He brought hope to Jews in many places. In the marshlands of White Russia, for example, the young Chaim Weizmann, destined to be first President of Israel, heard from his grandfather how Montefiore's carriage had been unharnessed and drawn in triumph through the city streets by the Jews of Vilna.

The Scots party met Montefiore twice. The first occasion was when they set out on horseback to explore the Mount of Olives and its surrounding area, and found it "far from being a solitude". Montefiore had pitched his tents on the hill and "multitudes of the Jews went out daily to lay their petitions before him". Sir Moses and Lady Montefiore received the unexpected Gentiles graciously, serving cake and wine, and a discussion followed on topics from the execrable state of the roads to the cultivation of vines, olives, and mulberries. Montefiore told his visitors of the wretched state of the substantial Jewish communities at Tiberias and Safed in Galilee (which Bonar and McCheyne were later to see at first hand), plundered by Arabs and the Druse and suffering from the aftermath of the great earthquake of 1837. "He conversed freely on the state of the land", wrote Bonar, "the miseries of the Jews, and the fulfilment of prophecy." Montefiore also agreed with the Scots that the Bible was the best guide-book to the Holy Land.

The second encounter was at the foot of Mount Carmel. The parts of Palestine through which the Scots had passed had

been visited by plague and there was compulsory quarantine,
including fumigation of books and papers, for those going to
Acre and beyond. During the week of enforced idleness
Montefiore's party ran into the same detention and Sir Moses
and the Scots exchanged courtesies and, up to a point, opinions. He and Dr Keith went for walks along the beach
discussing the "prophecies that had been fulfilled in the
desolations of the land..... But he positively declined all
reference to the New Testament." However he sent a present
of a fine water-melon, followed by two bottles of local wine
from the convent on Mount Carmel. Bonar allowed himself
a mild joke in the diary: "If this was a fair sample of that famous
wine it must have lost much of its excellence since the days of
Hosea." The dubious flavour was blamed on the use of tarred
thread to sew wineskins.

A few weeks before Sir Moses had found Mehemet Ali in
Cairo reasonably responsive to a plan for the establishment of
a company to lease land in Palestine to settle Jews in "100 or
200 villages", to enjoy their religion "in a manner which is
impossible in Europe". He was to find much less encouragement when power returned to the Sultan in Constantinople,
though his interest sustained and revived Jewish community
life in Jerusalem and has a lasting memorial in the Montefiore
village, looking across to Mount Zion, and the windmill
which remains both a landmark and a monument. But, as
Bonar noted later, it was to take four months to haul the parts
of the windmill from the coast up to Jerusalem, such were the
roads in this outlying Turkish province.

It is understandable that Zion-minded Christians like the
Scots of 1839 or the great Earl of Shaftesbury get little
recognition either from modern Orthodox Jewry or from the
secular Zionists of Israel. Sadly even Montefiore can be treated
rather patronisingly by the Zionists, who have all the fervour
of European nationalism and a tendency to substitute doctri-
naire ideology for religious dogma. These aspirations 20 years
before the birth of Theodor Herzl tend to be described, for
example by the gifted but very anti-evangelical American
historian, Barbara Tuchman, as "premature Zionism".

But it could reasonably be argued that political Zionism,
for good or ill or a mixture of the two, was made possible by

the mood of this earlier generation. It led both to the consol-
idation and extension of the modest Jewish presence in the
land and to the widespread acceptance in Western Europe and
even Russia of the possibility of Jewish colonisation, even
(were the Ottoman Empire to crumble) of some kind of
leading role for the Jews in Palestine.

Some of that discussion, then and later, was based on a
sketchy knowledge of the realities of Palestine as well as a
failure to appreciate the new forces which Turkish decline
would eventually release among the Arabs. Bonar and
McCheyne were no more perceptive than most Europeans
about the future of the Arabic-speaking peoples, but they were
extremely thorough in their inquiry into the condition of the
Jews and their observation of the state of the country. Like
other travellers, including many uninterested in biblical prophecy, they recorded the decay, neglect, and evidence of former
cultivation which they encountered.

But they did not give the impression of an empty land and
Bonar was later to write a wonderfully vivid summary of the
crops and seasons of the land in his book *Palestine for the
Young*. Their report noted the fertility of Samaria where even
in June there were reapers busy in the fields, camels laden with
sheaves, and lively treading and winnowing in the villages.

The Scots report put the population of Palestine at somewhere under 200,000. Other less conservative estimates tend
to be rather higher, but Bonar and McCheyne made the best
they could of information from consuls, missionaries, and
other contacts, among them Montefiore. But the Scots were
also conservative in their estimate of the Jewish population,
which they put at between 10,000 and 12,000, not more than
7 per cent of the total. In this case most of the estimates of
numbers and descriptions of the Jewish population were
backed by personal observation.

At Hebron they heard there were 80 German and Polish
Jews and had a friendly conversation over sherbet and water
with a blind rabbi who had been 50 years in the country. They
noted the graceful dress of the Jewish women but the poor
condition of the two synagogues. At the Tomb of Othniel
they plucked hyssop from crevices and thought of Solomon,

who spoke of trees ranging from the cedar of Lebanon to "the hyssop that grows out of the wall" (1 Kings 4.33).

At Nablus in Samaria Bonar joined in the synagogue worship of about 50 Jews and spoke afterwards to some of them in Italian or German. He also "engaged a very affable Jew" to take him along the Vale of Sychar to see Jacob's Well, where Jesus spoke to the Samaritan woman, and Joseph's Tomb, where Jews frequently visited. There Bonar found many Hebrew sentences inscribed on the walls. A few of the Nablus congregation were "natives of Sychar" - the name by which the Scots called the whole Nablus or Shechem area, and not just the nearby village of Askar often identified with it. But others of the Jews were from Spain or Russia.

Apart from the Jewish quarter of Jerusalem, Bonar and McCheyne found the main concentration of Jews in Galilee, where (with significant later results) they suggested that a Scots mission might take advantage of summer in the hills and the mild winter climate by the Sea of Galilee. Tiberias had three synagogues for European Ashkenazim and two for Eastern Sephardic Jews; Safed two for each community "and six of those places for study called *Yisvioth*". Near Safed the Scots also heard for the only occasion on their visit of a village where Jews cultivated the land "like *fellahs*".

Many of the Jewish communities they encountered were both old and poor. "There is always an influx", they were told, "but then the mortality is great and the number that come do no more than supply the places of those cut off." This was put down to change of climate "at the advanced period of life in which many come" as well as overcrowding in bad housing conditions. Some of the Jews were shopkeepers, others hawkers and pedlars. A few were workmen, though other sources suggest that most of the artisans in Jerusalem able to meet European needs were probably Jewish.

The number of times in which the Scots reported using German in conversation, especially in Galilee, indicates the substantial presence of Ashkenazim among the Jews of Palestine even in 1839. The opposite linguistic extreme in the Jewish community was an encounter between McCheyne and a Jewish boy who as yet spoke nothing but Arabic. But in their assessment of the linguistic problems facing future Scots missionaries Bonar and McCheyne provide an interesting footnote to the history of Hebrew in Palestine. Modern Hebrew is a later creation, and there is no disputing its importance in the shaping of Zionist nationalism and the creation of the modern Israeli sense of nationality. However even in 1839 the Scots reported:

> The Hebrew is the most necessary language for one who labours among the Jews of this country, and it is spoken chiefly in the Spanish way ....Arabic is not as absolutely necessary as Hebrew. All Jews in Palestine speak Hebrew, but then they often attach a meaning to the words that is not the true meaning or grammatical sense, so that it is absolutely necessary to know the vernacular tongue in order that you and they understand the same thing by the words employed.

All Jews were said to know a little Italian for their dealings with Westerners; but Hebrew, it seems, was already a *lingua franca* of sorts for Jews' dealings with each other, as well as with some biblically minded visitors.

But it should not be thought that the Scots' enthusiasm for things Jewish in any way diluted the intensity of their Christian experience of the Holy Land. They were not much concerned with shrines built on "holy places" and neither the first nor the last Christian pilgrims to be unimpressed by the Church of the Holy Sepulchre. It awakened in their minds no reverence but feelings "only painful and revolting". Galilee was a different matter, and at Gethsemane they meditated apart on Christ's sacrifice for them and then joined in prayer.

There are, however, two footnotes to ecumenical history that should be added to an account of their visit. The first is that in the Holy Land even these most dedicated evangelical Calvinists reflect some of the cultural affinities that Western Christians, whatever their doctrinal background, tend to feel with each other in the Holy Land, simply because they are Westerners in an Eastern country. One obvious, if minor example is agreement on the date of Easter. Another, very marked in Victorian times, was Westerners' ability to converse after a fashion with each other by pooling their knowledge of European languages and supplementing it with some Latin. Communication with native Christians was more difficult. Westerners were separated in many assumptions, customs (for example those governing social relations between the sexes), and ways of thought not only from Palestine's Muslim majority but from most of the local Christians.

Against this background Victorian Protestants and Roman Catholics, even though they were acutely aware of their differences and exchanged rather reserved courtesies, sometimes found unexpected affinities. For example at Jacob's Well Bonar and McCheyne, both zealous Protestants even by the standards of their time, even found a Latin "Romish hymn" about the weariness of Jesus "peculiarly impressive".

The second ecumenical footnote is that the report and its aftermath qualify assumptions about the rivalry and suspicion of the time between different Protestant denominations. Far from insisting on a Scots missionary presence in Jerusalem, the Kirk deliberately avoided a duplication of effort. Bonar and McCheyne suggested it might devote its main attention to Galilee, which it eventually did, though the plans for Scots Jewish missions were affected by the Disruption and diverted by the opportunity which the two older members of the delegation, Black and Keith, discovered in Budapest.- thanks to the favour of the German Protestant wife of the Habsburg Palatine or viceroy. As the result of the Disruption and this diversion the most immediate Presbyterian follow-up to Bonar and McCheyne was probably that of the Irish Presbyterians who started work in Syria and Lebanon - and whose missionaries' letters home reveal the ferocity of conflict among Christians, Muslims, and Druse that TV reports from the Lebanon showed so vividly nearly 150 years later. The Scots Kirk did not even build a Scots church to serve English-speaking Reformed Christianity in Jerusalem for nearly a century, and then only in very special circumstances.

That attitude may have been possible because, long before ecumenical structures began to take shape, the ecumenical spirit was apparent in 1839. There was a congregation of only 14 for the Lord's Supper in an upper room in the house of the British Consul, Mr Young, on the Scots expedition's last Sunday in Jerusalem. Two were Christian Jews, one an Arab

Christian from Nazareth, drawn to Protestant ways by American missionaries. The English Prayer Book service was read by the Danish-born Anglican missionary Mr Nicolayson and there were no barriers to inter-communion. After Nicolayson had preached, Dr Keith joined him in administering the bread and wine. In the evening Bonar expounded the text "In my Father's house are many mansions" and the little congregation "joined in the prayer that Israel might soon have their solemn feasts restored to them". It broke up after singing the last part of Psalm 116, about taking the cup of salvation and praising the Lord in the midst of Jerusalem. But the Scots were up early the next morning to hear the Hebrew liturgy at the English mission-house.

There they joined two Christian Jews in the Hebrew responses as Mr Nicolayson read the service, and they rejoiced in hearing "the holy tongue made use of in believing prayer in the name of Jesus". Later in the day they went by narrow and lonely streets, with a Jew as their guide, to look at the Western Wall and reflect on biblical prophecies about the stones of the Temple.

In the evening they visited all six synagogues of Jerusalem at the time of prayer, finding (as it was an ordinary working day) that those present were mainly children learning to read. They then called on a rabbi who showed them the view from his house, and they noted that his roof had the railing or battlement commanded by the law in Deuteronomy 22.8. On the next day the Scots took their farewell of Jerusalem, feeling they had shared in an inexpressibly precious communion of the saints.

They went home with a sense, in Bonar's later words, that the Jews would still be chosen for great things and special purposes. "When it is to be we cannot tell, though many signs encourage us to believe that the time to favour Zion is very near."

He lived till 1892, the year the railway reached Jerusalem from Jaffa, preaching till the last week of his life and struggling from his deathbed to remind his Glasgow congregation that the next Sunday's collection was for Jewish missions. He was the brother of the "prince of Scottish hymn-writers", Horatius

Bonar, and source of Christian names for the son of the manse
who became Prime Minister, Andrew Bonar Law.

McCheyne returned to the exhilaration of revival in
Dundee but had less than four years to live. Bonar wrote his
biography. He also ensured publication of McCheyne's ser-
mons and some of his other work, including a poem which
commemorates the expedition of 1839 and captures both its
mood and some of its most intense experiences:

> Though Zion like a field be ploughed,
> And Salem covered with a cloud;
> Though briers and thorns are tangled o'er
> Where vine and olive twined before;
> Though turbaned Moslem treads the gate,
> And Judah sits most desolate;
> Their nets o'er Tyre the fishers spread,
> And Carmel's top is withered:
> Yet still these waters clasp the shore
> As kindly as they did before!
>
> Such is thy love to Judah's race,
> A deep unchanging tide of grace.
>
> Though scattered now at thy command
> They pine away in every land,
> With trembling heart and failing eyes,
> And deep the veil on Israel lies;
> Yet still thy word thou canst not break,
> Beloved for their fathers' sake.

# 3 THE VIENNESE LADY, THE ARTIST, AND THE HEBREW BISHOP

*IDA PFEIFFER'S JOURNEY, WILLIAM BARTLETT'S SKETCHES, AND BISHOP ALEXANDER'S CATHEDRAL*

On a mild March morning in 1842 a Viennese lady in her forties took a cab to the Kaisersmühle, near the site of the modern International Centre, to board the paddle-steamer going down the Danube. Most of her fellow-passengers were only going to Pressburg, now the Slovakian Bratislava, though one didn't make it. The police, urged on by a creditor, asked him to leave to discuss a large debt which he had forgotten to settle before planning to sail for Hungary.

Ida Pfeiffer meant to change steamers at Budapest and go much farther than Hungary. She was so determined to go to Jerusalem that those who met her assumed she was a frustrated nun, driven by some intense religious devotion to take the risks of travelling to Palestine as an unescorted woman. In fact she was beginning a career as a compulsive voyager, eventually paying for round-the-world travel by writing about it. Although she was a Christian, she was not a pilgrim in the ordinary sense, for her primary motive was to see new countries. She did not travel to find God, for she knew he would go with her; nor did she make devotion an excuse in trying to explain matters to her bewildered family.

Frau Pfeiffer was a determined lady whose independent outlook had been strengthened in adversity. Her marriage to a lawyer in Lemberg (Lvov) had been broken by his reckless and spendthrift habits. Only after she came into a legacy and her two sons were grown-up was she able to divert her talent for saving and scraping from a fight for survival to a struggle for independence and to achieve that "desire and dream of a lifetime", a trip to the Holy Land.

In travelling to Palestine - not quite sure how to get there from Constantinople - she exercised a right of private judgment that might have seemed ultra-Protestant, for family and friends tried to dissuade her from the trip. In fact she was a Roman Catholic of rather conventional piety and no rebel in doctrinal matters, though at a personal level she got on well with the German and British Protestants whom she encountered on the voyage, and who on occasion gave her vital assistance.

Ida Pfeiffer was plain in her looks - small and rather bony - and by the standards of Vienna rather dowdy. The very ordinariness of her previous life and her ideas makes her extraordinary journey all the more interesting. Her journal gives a plain view of the journey to the Holy Land uncoloured by any scholarly, political, or theological insight. Her record of her visit is a reminder that, amid the excitements of political change, scholarly research, and prophetic insights, Palestine, even in the nineteenth century, offered a unique experience for ordinary people whom ambition or circumstances allowed to travel there.

Among them were Roman Catholics of various nationalities, Russian peasants, British officers taking a detour on the journey to or from India, and eventually Protestant tourists on Cook's tours. Few of them in 1842, however, were women on their own, without even the guides and servants that male Westerners were advised to regard as essential. And few of those who wrote books needed to watch their expenses as the frugal Frau Pfeiffer had to do.

The Danube route to Constantinople was tedious and uncomfortable rather than adventurous; and when she reached the Golden Horn most of her six weeks there were spent in rather conventional sightseeing. The main interest in her diary there - an asset also found in her Holy Land narrative - lies in her access to women's life in places closed to Western men. But the confusing advice she received in the Turkish capital shows how unstable the Ottoman Empire still was. A priest told her the only safe course was to wait all summer and join the Greek pilgrim caravan in the autumn. A returned pilgrim told hair-raising tales of danger and adventure. Sober witnesses warned of unrest and plague in Lebanon. Told that she must wear men's clothing, she decided not to deny her sex. She adopted a very personal costume of a blouse and Eastern ladies' *Beinkleider* - German for baggy trousers - under a shawl-like head-dress, with the ensemble topped by a wide straw hat. On the other points she was so confused that she decided to sail for Beirut on an Austrian ship (manned by Italians and Dalmatians) and see what was possible there.

Beirut was an ordeal. There was no room at the inns, though a sympathetic hotel-keeper let her stay with his wife and family while word went round of the Frankish lady anxious to reach Jerusalem. She waited in intense and stifling heat, with nowhere to change her clothes, while the children chattered and scampered noisily around; she was unable to communicate with them or their mother, who spoke only Arabic. She noted that the custom of the country was that "the wife does nothing but play with children or chat to the woman next door, while the man looks after the kitchen, the cellar, and all the shopping."

Fortunately help was at hand. An English Protestant artist and writer, with whom she had struck up shipboard conversation in French on the Sea of Marmora, heard of her plight and offered her a passage on an Arab *felucca* or rigged open bark that had agreed to take him to Caesarea in Palestine. He was on his second trip to the Middle East and dissented from the general view that Westerners must depend on local guides.

The *felucca* was neither clean nor comfortable, smelled strongly of fish, offered a choice of lying down on the boat's ribs or its ballast of sand and shingle, and had no privacy or shelter. But it sailed in the right direction. Frau Pfeiffer and her English protector spread their cloaks on their baggage and took a place of honour separate from the other passengers - including one who wanted to be as separate as possible. He had bought a young slave girl at the Constantinople market and was trying to keep her cooped up and immune from curious eyes.

The attempt to land at Caesarea went wrong, for there were no horses to be had, and the next stop was Jaffa, where Frau Pfeiffer managed to lodge and board with the Austrian Consul who also represented France. He claimed to speak French, but seemed to suffer from loss of linguistic memory, so that conversation had to be in a kind of Italian which the Viennese lady found hard to follow, because there were so many Greek words in the dialect.

Her English protector had arranged horses for the journey across the Plain of Sharon, "the very picture of a fruitful and inhabited region", and into the Judean hills. This was the main road for Western travellers but Frau Pfeiffer's diary testifies to its discomforts and hazards. She was dizzy as well as weary in the heat of the plain and could hardly stay on her horse. When they stopped to rest they had to buy dirty, muddy, and tepid water. Later on, at Kiryat Jearim, where the Ark of the Covenant had once rested and which has been identified with Emmaus, they were uncertain whether the protection money paid to the local sheikh (included in the bill for sour milk, honey, cucumbers, eggs, and olives) covered the other Arabs on the route. For safety they set out on the last stage at midnight and reached Jerusalem's Jaffa Gate at 5.30 in the morning. They had to wait there for another half hour for the Turkish garrison to open the gate.

"It was the finest morning of my life", wrote Ida Pfeiffer after she had been safely delivered to the Franciscans who ran the pilgrim hospice, where among the Spanish and Italian monks she was delighted to find a Viennese. Safely based there, she began a conventional round of the holy places and spent a night in the Church of the Holy Sepulchre, where "an old Spanish woman who lives like a nun" acted as companion for women pilgrims. The noise from many quarters as "more disturbing than uplifting". At midnight the different services began. "The Greeks and Armenians beat and hammered on boards or metal bars. The Latins played the organ or sang and prayed loudly, while the priests of other sects sang and cried. It was a most unharmonious noise." But Frau Pfeiffer stayed to hear several Masses and at eight in the morning asked the Turkish guards to unbar the door to let her back to the pilgrim-house at the Casa Nuova.

She also noted things which more exalted travellers were often too busy to record. The food at the hospice was adequate but monotonous, especially the roast, boiled, and pickled mutton, for in summer there was no beef or veal to be had. On the frequent fast-day menus the lentil soup and omelettes went

with a choice of hot or cold dried fish. She also sounded rather
tired of cucumbers.

She sometimes recorded naively what she was told. This
applied when she visited holy places and saw relics, and also in
the Casa Nuova. No questions were asked about religious
belief - which was true, though visitors' adherence soon
became obvious enough. In the hospice there was no tariff.
Visitors made voluntary gifts - "much, little, or nothing" - and
could stay for up to a month. Other visitors saw this rather
differently. "There is no fixed price, but an English traveller
is expected to give a rather handsome compliment for the
accommodation thus afforded", wrote a Protestant who lodged
at the Casa Nuova at the same time - the artist who had secured
her passage from Beirut.

Before she returned home to Vienna for Christmas, by
way of Damascus and Egypt, Frau Pfeiffer also did the rounds
of the main holy places outside Jerusalem. One of them
involved a four-hour trip in a party across the bare Judean hills
to the Greek monastery of Mar Saba, a very ancient foundation which had been plundered in 1835 but restored in 1840
with Russian help. It is still a tourist and pilgrim attraction
today. "Pull bell cord in door at foot of ramp", says Father
Murphy-O'Connor in his authoritative modern guide, before
adding: "No women admitted."

So it was in 1842. The monks saw the cavalcade approaching and the door opened at the first knock or pull on the bell
cord. In rode the gentlemen, among them four Central
European counts and a baron, then the senior servants, then
the hired Arabs and Bedouin. But not Ida Pfeiffer. Barred from
the monastery, she feared she was condemned to a night in the
open in a desolate country when a lay brother appeared
carrying a ladder. He pointed to a tower outside the walls,
conducted her there, used the ladder to take her to a room in
the tower, and then removed the ladder. It was not clear
whether this was to deter robbers, monks and other male
visitors, or the lady herself, lest she make another bid to enter
the monastery.

Some of the gentlemen of the party appear to have shown
a cavalier indifference to this segregation and incarceration,
and others not to have noticed in time. Among the more

chivalrous was the English artist who had seen Frau Pfeiffer
safely from Beirut to Jerusalem. He was, he says, already in the
pilgrim apartment when he realised that "the German lady"was
missing. He went out to the tower to be assured that she would
be all right for the night, even without a guard at the foot of
the building. He also reported that he had ensured she got her
dinner. On that point Frau Pfeiffer's testimony differs only
slightly. The monks did bring her food, she said, but it was
really only a snack.

     In her account of the journey Frau Pfeiffer did not name
the English Protestant artist who helped her reach Jerusalem
and did his best in face of the misogynist monks of Mar Saba.
But he can be identified because he has his own importance in
the literary history of pilgrimage and the artistic history of
Palestine. The stories of the passage from Beirut and the
incident at Mar Saba are told in two totally separate narratives.
Frau Pfeiffer gave him an honourable mention in *Reise einer
Wienerin in das Heilige Land* - a Viennese lady's journey to the
Holy Land. He published a narrative of his travels with his
sketches, and mentioned in passing a German lady travelling
on her own, "a quiet enthusiast who gave no-one any trouble,
enjoyed everything in silence, and never uttered a murmur
during the heat and fatigue of our journey".

He was William Henry Bartlett, a Londoner who visited the
Holy Land three times. His most important works were
*Walks about Jerusalem* - the fruit of the 1842 journey on which
he helped Ida Pfeiffer - and *Jerusalem Revisited*, which he had
sent to his publisher before taking ship home in 1854. He
never saw it in print, for he died aged 45 on the voyage from
Malta to Marseilles and was buried at sea.

     Bartlett was one of two notable British artists who visited
the Holy Land at roughly the same time and whose work has
found favour in modern Israel, where his books on Jerusalem
have been republished. The other was the far better-known
Edinburgh man, David Roberts, a considerable as well as a
fashionable painter who toured the Middle East in 1839.
Roberts rose to an eminence far removed from his humble
artistic beginnings painting scenery for Edinburgh and Glasgow theatres. He travelled to the Royal Academy by way of

Drury Lane, Covent Garden, and a feeling for romantic landscape and architecture - first in Spain and then the Middle East. In modern times he is to be found on calendars, picture-postcards, and attractive reproductions that make him seem even more colourful than he was. He is much in favour in modern Israel but his work was also used when most of the pilgrim and tourist attractions were in Jordanian hands before 1967. He is at his most striking painting ruins and rituals. His human figures, however, seem to come out of the Arabian Nights rather than the dusty, scruffy, and far from odourless Holy Land of his time. He has also been accused - for example in Norman Macleod's comparison of his Sea of Galilee with Holman Hunt's - of taking liberties with the landscape.

There was, indeed a third British artist, the greatest of the three, who passed that way not long after Roberts and the year before Bartlett's dealings with Frau Pfeiffer. But Sir David Wilkie, a Scottish son of the manse, is remembered for the way he expressed in colour many aspects of Scottish life and character, and not least Scots Reformed religion. Even now that he is coming back into fashion - see for example the sympathetic and extended assessment in Duncan Macmillan's recent definitive history of Scottish art - Wilkie's last journey is almost forgotten. We can only guess what this great Christian artist would have done if he had been spared to reflect on what he had seen in the Holy Land. But the watercolour of a muleteer he employed for his journey from Jerusalem down to Jaffa (on show at the 1993 Edinburgh Festival) must have been almost his last work. Like Bartlett more than a decade later, he died on the voyage home.

As an artist Bartlett was not in the same class as Roberts or Wilkie. However he is probably a much better witness to the condition of the country than the romantic and spectacular Roberts. Like Roberts he found artistic fascination in ruins and remains but he also sketched some of the new buildings rising in Jerusalem and the narrow vennels - the old Scots word is very apt - of the crowded and sometimes squalid city. Equally important, he turned out to be a good journalistic as well as artistic observer, with the additional benefit that his two main books demonstrate the very considerable changes that gathered momentum in the Holy Land, and especially Jerusalem, between the early 1840's and the Crimean War.

There are other vivid descriptions from travellers of the time, such as one by the Anglo-Irishman Eliot Warburton, who in 1847 summed up the condition of Jerusalem: "Zion offers only privations to the pilgrim's body, solemn reflections for his thoughts, awe for his soul. Her palaces are ruins, her hostels are dreary convents, her chief boast and triumph is a sepulchre." But Bartlett combined the visitor's excitement with the perspectives of experience over 20 years.

Because Bartlett made three visits to the Holy Land (the first had been in 1834-35) he noted changes in a way that single-visit travellers could not and the few long-term European and American residents perhaps did not. For example in 1853 he found that the monks at Ramleh (which medieval tradition claimed as Arimathea and Israelis call Ramla) were becoming less hospitable to Protestants and thought he owed his admission to his travelling-companion, a Frenchman who had shared an especially *"mauvais quart d'heure"* in a choppy landing at Jaffa. In Jerusalem he found there were now two main inns catering for Europeans, the "Mediteranean" and the "Maltese". Their rate was from 35 to 50 piastres a day (up to ten shillings) with drinkable local wine included and bottled ale and porter as well as spirits available as extras.

He was able to note more signficant changes. Jerusalem, he said was "rapidly springing up into new life", even though half the old city area still lay desolate. There were European shops, three tailors, good supplies in the markets, "and of late cows' milk is to be had". He noted a new bank, consulates, and fine houses - as well as the sign of Sir Moses Montefiore's philanthropy, the new Jewish dispensary. He also saw more of Jewish life than most Western Christians could expect, and in his book about the 1842 visit sketched in words as well as pictures what he saw of life in the Jewish quarter, including a visit to a Jewish family where he found the women, unlike Oriental Christians as well as Muslims, "seemed on a perfect footing of equality", and even in the presence of a Christian stranger "chatted and laughed away without intermission". But he lamented that most of the Jewish population seemed to be supported in pious pauperism rather than through commerce and crafts. Other Christian visitors were less sympathetic. The great novelist W.M. Thackeray, who was in Jerusalem in 1844 during a Mediterreanean tour, found the Jewish quarter "pre-eminent in filth" and thought the Valley of Jehoshaphat and the Jewish burial grounds "the most ghastly sight I have seen anywhere in the world".

Although he was an artist and not an evangelist, Bartlett was also close to another significant development in Jerusalem: the foundation of the Anglican bishopric. When he conducted Ida Pfeiffer there in 1842 his main contact in the city was his friend J.W. Johns, British vice-consul and at that time architect of the proposed Anglican cathedral of St James on Mount Zion not far from the Jaffa Gate, on which work was about to start. Indeed although Bartlett lodged at the Franciscan pilgrim-house he appears to have enjoyed Johns' hospitality at meals and not the mutton-dominated diet the Viennese lady found so monotonous.

The story of that bishopric is one of the strangest episodes in modern Christian history. Its origins lie in missions to the Jews and in co-operation between the English and Prussian Churches and the British and Prussian Governments. The aim of the scheme, formally sponsored in diplomacy by the King of Prussia but dear to the heart of Lord Shaftesbury, was to create a common framework for English and German missions in the Holy Land as well as a focal point around which an Evangelical Hebrew Church could be gathered. Its history provoked tensions in the Church of England between High Church and Evangelical parties (because the Prussian Union Church incorporating Lutheran and Reformed traditions did not fit high views of "apostolic succession") and it could be argued that by all human standards it set back both the reconciliation of Christians and Jews and co-operation between British and German Protestants. It sorely troubled W.E. Gladstone, it may have helped J.H. Newman down the slippery slope to Rome, and it provoked good Christians to talk nonsense, as when E.B. Pusey complained of the Church of England "holding communication with those that are without the Church".

Nothing went according to plan. By the 1870's Anglicans and Germans decided to go their separate ways and the

modern Episcopal Church in the Holy Land is Arab, not
Jewish. The legacy of the bishopric in education, the great
achievement of the second bishop, the Swiss-born Samuel
Gobat, belongs to Palestinian rather than denominational
history. St George's, the Anglican Cathedral in modern
Jerusalem, is not the one Johns hoped to build and about
which Bartlett wrote in both his Jerusalem books. The high
profile of the mission and the bishopric, and their emphasis on
speaking "to the Jew first" stimulated both Jewish activity -
much of it made possible by Montefiore's support - and Jewish
rabbinical hostility. There was also friction with the Greek
and Armenian patriarchates, reflecting an uncertainty in
Anglican Evangelical attitudes about how best to help their
people.

The cathedral about which Bartlett wrote was built, but in
a new and modest version. It is today's Christ Church near the
Jaffa Gate, with the Hebrew inscription on its Communion
Table as a reminder both of the continuing Jewish mission
connection and of its origins. This is the church where the first
bishop, the Jewish-born Michael Solomon Alexander, laid the
foundation stone in 1842, though when W.M. Thackeray
visited in 1844 the "polyglot services" (with Alexander preaching in German every Sunday) were still in the mission-house.
But as Bartlett noted even in his 1842 book, the scheme had
run into trouble. What he called the imbecile and barbarous
Turkish Government - in reality weak but devious - had
insisted that the scheme for an imposing cathedral be modified
into one which made the building part of the British Consulate. Later the quarrelling extended to the sponsors themselves
and Johns was sacked as architect, leaving Bartlett to fill his last
book with lamentations about what might have been.

By then Bishop Alexander had died and had been succeeded by Samuel Gobat, a German nominee of French-Swiss
origin, whose personal qualities ensured the troubled survival
of the bishopric in its joint form for his working lifetime. (It
then became exclusively Anglican, first English and eventually Arab.) The actual minister of Christ Church was the Mr
Nicolayson who had so heartily welcomed Bonar and
McCheyne back in 1839.

Bartlett was left to reflect on indirect, though considerable, changes produced by the English mission and the mini-cathedral which affirmed its presence. It had stimulated education by example and emulation; it had even challenged "the stagnant torpor of ignorance and sloth that has so long settled over the Eastern Churches"; it had shown that "wherever the English establish themselves they never fail to introduce a higher standard of comfort, improved sanitary regulations, a stimulus to industry and agriculture." The local Arab peasants, he thought, were coming to see that their interests were interwoven with those of the Franks.

From today's standpoint Bartlett's enthusiasm for the progress of European civilisation, which he equated with British influence, may seem naive or complacent or both. But it recognised changes that were gathering momentum, and the direction though not the destination of events. Among the immediate results was an increase in the scale as well as a change in the character of Protestant pilgrimage to the Holy Land. It could become scheduled and fairly secure, with some of the pleasures of tourism mingled with spiritual experience, shallow or profound according to the character and interest of the pilgrim-tourist.

And among Bartlett's journalistic and rather hurried observations, unrevised because of his death, there stands out a mere aside which future events give an importance he himself can scarcely have recognised. The Jews, he noted, did not speak of the Holy Land in the same sense as Christians, though they used the phrase for particular sacred places within it. They spoke instead of the Land of Israel.

# 4 QUEEN VICTORIA'S MAN GOES EAST

*NORMAN MACLEOD'S SPIRITUAL GUIDE TO PILGRIMAGE*

A modern Israeli publisher of Bartlett's *Walks about Jerusalem* estimates that about a million pilgrims visited the Holy Land during the nineteenth century. The great majority of them came in the second half of the century, when a revolution in travel coincided with a new security for Western travellers.

Most of them probably kept diaries of some sort and many wrote books. Between 1840 and the end of the century there was an annual average of about 40 books on Holy Land travel published in Britain. In some of them accounts of travel mingled with scholarship as well as religious devotion, for example in two notable Anglican books, Dean Stanley's *Sinai and Palestine* and Canon Tristram's account of the journeys which made him an authority on flora and fauna. Such books, like that of Bonar and McCheyne (which by 1848 had sold 24,000 copies), were immensely popular and successful.

There was also a wide range of books of varied merits and pretensions, with the most meritorious sometimes the least pretentious. Those Christians who fulfilled that "desire and dream of a lifetime" to visit the Holy Land seem to have had both an inner compulsion to record their intensity of experience and a sense of duty to share it with those they left at home: families, congregations, and admiring readers.

Not surprisingly there is a sameness about many of the books from the travellers, especially the vast majority who made only one relatively short trip. Books by those who lived in the country for a more extended term are a different matter, whether in the immensely famous and successful popular scholarship of Thomson or in a forgotten little gem like *Syria and Palestine*, by Edward Jonas, who had returned from Palestine after serving as a layman with the Anglican mission, and turned his diaries into a book some years later when he had been ordained and was rector of the Episcopal church in Kilmarnock. So, in a different way, are the relatively few books by those who travelled to the Middle East primarily to enhance a literary reputation or simply to write for profit, though the best-known names are not always the most satisfying reading. For example among the American visitors Mark Twain doesn't wear as well as Charles Dudley Warner, also a well-known writer in his day but not such a well-remembered one.

But the main body of diarists and journal-keepers followed pretty well the same route to the same places and recorded the travels in the same kind of narratives. When they reacted in different ways, this usually reflected theological and liturgical assumptions in which they were firmly set long before setting out on their pilgrimage. Some were also betrayed by the importance of their subject into a self-important style which exaggerated the literary tendencies of the time. They sermonised, they moralised, and they assumed that great themes demanded long words and elaborate descriptions.

Yet the best of them were very good; and the worst of them have something to contribute to the history both of travel and of religion.

A good example of the best sort of literary pilgrim, and an unfairly neglected one, is Norman Macleod, Queen Victoria's favourite chaplain. Macleod (1812-72) belonged to a famous Scottish ministerial family, six of whom were Moderators of the Kirk's General Assembly - among them his grandson George, founder of the Iona Community and eventually Lord MacLeod of Fuinary.

Norman Macleod was a great Victorian, friend and pastoral adviser of the Queen but both an establishment figure and a social reformer. He was one of the evangelicals who stayed within the Church of Scotland at the Disruption of 1843 and who revived it in the decades that followed. In Scotland he is still usually remembered as "Norman Macleod of the Barony", partly to distinguish him from namesakes in the clan, but also because of the impact his ministry made in mid-Victorian industrial Glasgow, where his city-centre Barony parish showed both the vigour and the squalor of the age.

Much of his wider influence came from his role as editor of the popular but high-quality London monthly magazine *Good Words*, in which he serialised throughout 1865, as *Eastward*, an account of a visit to the Middle East. The other main serial attraction of the magazine that year was Charles Kingsley's *Hereward, the Last of the English*. Its most striking unscheduled item was an editorial lament for "the martyred President", unusual for its emphasis on Abraham Lincoln's Kentuckian birth and Southern connections.

Perhaps it is because it began life as journalism - high-class, but still journalism - that *Eastward* has a freshness and lack of pretension rare in the pilgrim testimonies of that decade. Macleod insisted that he travelled free of the main concerns of many travellers of his time. He had not been sent to the Mediterranean for his health's sake. He had not been deputed "to undertake a missionary tour". And he did not mean to write a book "describing the East for the thousandth time, whether in the form of letters, tour, diary, sketches, thoughts, or pictures." But of course he changed his mind.

What emerged is at one level a very gifted communicator's simple acount of his voyage and his feelings. Studied more carefully, it yields a wealth of evidence about the dramatic changes that had come over the Holy Land in the 25 years since the visit of Bonar and McCheyne. It also has profound things to say, and lessons still worth teaching, about the relation of the pilgrimage experience to the Christian life.

Macleod set out eastward in February 1864, opting to reach Alexandria by train to Marseilles and onward by steamer rather than by the other choices of the time, the sea-voyage by Gibraltar and the quickest route, via Ancona on the Adriatic, already linked by rail to Turin. "Alexandria is the starting-point to Palestine for all travellers approaching it from the West." But it was also the starting-point, as with most tourist-pilgrims with sufficient leisure and means, for a subsidiary Egyptian tour to Cairo and the Red Sea. Victorian travellers, unlike most modern pilgrims, were not forced by their own budgets or other people's politics to see the Holy Land in isolation. And although they could be cavalier in their attitude to the ways of life as well as the way of government in Palestine, many of them were able to contrast the situation there not with Europe but with the more developed Muslim society in Egypt and sometimes with Constantinople, which then seemed the capital of the Islamic world. Many of them, including Macleod, also visited Damascus, where he saw the destruction left by the terrible anti-Christian riots of 1860, which had brought both massacre and devastation and widened the gap between Western Christendom and Islam. Despite this alienation and suspicion, nineteenth-century Christian pilgrims were still able to contrast a great city of the Arab world with the impresssion given by Jerusalem - sacred to three religions, yet a dirty and backward provincial town nonetheless. The twentieth-century traveller has found it easier to reach Palestine, but not to move freely between the State of Israel and its neighbours.

But although Alexandria had become the starting-point, the actual port of entry to Palestine in 1864 remained at Jaffa, except when the weather forced ships to carry on to the all-weather but inconvenient landing at Haifa. In sailing to Jaffa from Alexandria, Macleod encountered another sign of the times: a Russian steamship line supplying slow passages from the Black Sea through the Bosphorus to the Eastern Mediterranean. The ship was comfortable enough but unable to reach eight knots. It was also crowded, though with contrasting groups of passengers.

Although one of the main reasons for the Russian shipping connection was the growth of Russian peasant pilgrimage to the Holy Land, most of the pilgrim-passengers at this season were Muslims on their way home from Mecca. They filled most of the deck space, most of them in the open, though half the quarter-deck had been tented in canvas to accommodate "the more aristocratic portion of the pilgrims". The Christians with cabins included not only Macleod's party, including his brother and his publisher, but a group of American missionaries and the deposed Duke of Modena, a ruler displaced by the recent wave of Italian revolutions. The Duke was credited not only with stimulating the Russians into ensuring "dignity and good dinners" but with the influence to ensure a landing at Jaffa and the shortest route to Jerusalem.

That choppy landing at Jaffa, where the local boats came a mile out to the ships, supplied an emotion to be recollected in the tranquillity of Holy Land memoirs. Some pilgrims were convinced that the Arab boatmen contrived to balance on the breakers until their victims agreed to a higher than originally contracted price. Macleod's memories were of thinking more than once of Jonah and then being dragged on to land. There followed an overpowering emotion - not about the holiness of the dry land but "to be delivered from the Philistines" who swarmed around the newly-landed travellers. He was delivered, of course, and stayed at the model farm run by a London-based mission "to provide labour for converted Jews", though its manager Dr Philip was also a medical missionary. The next day he admired the "marvellous richness, the orchard beauty" that made the neighbourhood seem a Promised Land and then saw the sights, notably the flat-roofed house which was claimed to be that of Simon the Tanner where (as Luke records in the Book of Acts) the Apostle Peter "tarried many days" and pondered the meaning of a vision.

Once a pilgrim-diarist had devoted one purple passage to the landing at Jaffa he had soon to summon up another to describe his dragoman and travel-arrangements. The Western traveller's dragoman - who was interpreter, guide, tour-treasurer and manager - was often an Arab Christian but Macleod's Hadji Ali Abu Halawy was (as his name implies) not only a Muslim but one who had gained status by a pilgrimage to Mecca. He had also gained favour in a very different city. Macleod took him on the recommendation of his friend Professor J.L. Porter of Belfast, author of an important book on Damascus-based travels and of Murray's guidebook to Syria and Palestine.

As late as 1924 Cook's *Traveller's Handbook to Palestine and Syria* was still insisting that it was practically impossible to travel independently in Palestine and that "a dragoman is absolutely essential, and it is incumbent on the traveller to see that he does not get into the hands of irresponsible Arabs and others whose only aim may be to get his money." In 1864 the dragomans were entering their golden age, for the country was secure enough to attract more Western visitors - mainly comfortably off - but alien and backward enough to pose difficulties.

There were still no railways and the only hotels were in Jerusalem and Jaffa. More important, there were no roads as the West knew them and, as Macleod said, "no wheeled vehicles, not even a wheelbarrow, from Dan to Beersheba". In addition to the dragoman there was a Nubian whom Macleod irreverently called the "Hadji's mate" and whose main responsibility was to act as waiter and personal attendant to the five Franks. Third in seniority came a cook who suffered intermittent pains "we shall not say where but intimately connected with his digestion". His afflictions healed, or at least relieved, from Macleod's medicine-chest, he expressed his gratitude by conferring on Queen Victoria's chaplain the additional honorific title of Hakim Pasha or chief physician. The other attendants comprised a master of horse with three subordinate muleteers to look after about ten pack-horses and mules. Among the baggage with which they were laden were the tents for the evening encampments, one of them a "mess tent" big enough to take a dinner table as well as three beds.

One of the duties of the dragoman was to handle the major problems of baksheesh - another favourite theme of the Holy Land travellers. Macleod was more restrained and objective on the subject than some more excitable pilgrims. It arose when the caravan, after a lunch-time halt near the site of the present Lod airport, made its first night-stop, set up camp on the first spur of the Judean hills, and enjoyed the kind of dinner which a good dragoman could provide - "soup, roast mutton, fowls, curry, excellent vegetables, a pudding, a good dessert, and *café noir*." But as usually happened, a Frankish camp drew a crowd from the neighbouring village. It "asked *baksheesh* and we distributed about sixpence among the tribe. They were satisfied." Probably the dragoman had made the principal arrangements with the sheikh.

Almost every hour, Macleod admitted, seemed to enlarge their knowledge of "this Eastern impost" which figures so prominently in Western travel memoirs. But Macleod was more philosophical about it than many travellers, protesting a little too much that it was really no more than a sorely oppressed people's equivalent of tipping: "I fear that it is an almost universal custom."

His relaxed approach perhaps conceals the extent to which nineteenth-century pilgrims now encountered a more relaxed situation, at least on the coast and on the main routes to Jerusalem, than their precedessors. Later on the trip, on the way from Hebron to Bethlehem, Macleod and his party prepared their pistols "notwithstanding our being minus both powder and shot" when they were accosted by six horsemen, whom they feared were about to plunder the baggage. But after the six sought and were denied *baksheesh*, apparently content with a performance on a musical snuff-box which Macleod produced on such occasions, it turned out they were a detachment of Turkish police. "So much for the fears and hairsbreadth escapes of travellers", he reflected. Matters remained rather different, as Tristram's book makes clear, around the Dead Sea, while the evangelical canoeist John MacGregor was to be kidnapped for ransom on the upper waters of the Jordan when he set out to sail his *Rob Roy* down to the Sea of Galilee in 1868. And long after the road to Jerusalem was safe, Christian travellers and their guides had to be circumspect around Nablus, though there the problem was not banditry but the strength of Muslim feeling. Yet the decaying Turkish Empire increasingly depended on the good will of the powerful European consuls and had to muster such resources as it had to protect their people. Jonas noted that this affected not only the condition of the Christians but of some of the Jews. Ashkenazim from Germany, Austria, and Russia claimed consular protection and were less oppressed than the Sephardic Jews, mainly subjects of the Sultan.

Macleod's dragoman felt secure enough to be able to meet the party's wish to reach Jerusalem by the more northerly and less direct of the two ways to Jerusalem from the coast, though discussion of the route still involved "the probability of pitching among civil neighbours or finding a sheikh who may be known to the dragoman." This rough but spectacular road led close by Gibeon (el Jib) to the most dominant of the hills around Jerusalem, Nebi Samwil. It is an area rich in biblical and other historical associations. Joshua spared the Gibeonites during the conquest of Canaan but (as related in Joshua 9) made them hewers of wood and drawers of water. When Saul sought to destroy them, in violation of Joshua's covenant,

Israel felt its guilt in three years of famine and David allowed the men of Gibeon to hang seven of Saul's sons and grandsons on "the mountain of the Lord" at the beginning of the barley-harvest (2 Samuel 21.9). Nebi Samwil may have been the great high place where Solomon offered sacrifice for the gift of wisdom, though it is tradition rather than history which makes it the site of Samuel's tomb. This hill-top, from which both the Mediterranean and the trans-Jordanian hills of Moab can be seen, is certainly the site from which Crusaders gazed down on Jerusalem, and the key strategic point whose capture by the Lowland Scots Territorials in 1917 settled the fate of the city and ended an era in Palestine.

The journey in 1864 was a slow one, and the riders learned that the safest technique was to go easy on the bridle and let the horses find their own safe footing among the loose stones, slippery limestone ledges, and river-beds that served as road-way. That leisurely pace seems to have inspired some of Macleod's best meditations on Palestine, some of them fit for a spiritual guide-book for today's pilgrims to a country whose cities, plains, and valleys have changed so much.

It was the smallness of the country, so much of it visible from Nebi Samwil, and its contrasts which impressed Macleod. He admitted not finding the romantic beauty "and look of a second Paradise which one has sometimes heard in descriptions of it from the pulpit." But, he said, he did not feel disappointed with Palestine, for it was the greatest poem he ever read, full of tragic grandeur and the sweetest hymns: "I did not look for beauty and therefore was not surprised at its absence. But I did look for the battle scenes - for the Marathon and Thermopylae - of the world's civilisation, and for the earthly stage on which real men of flesh and blood, but full of the spirit of the Living God, played out their grand parts ....I found it no other than I looked for, to my ceaseless joy and thankgiving", he wrote.

> I left the top of Nebi Samwil with devoutest thanksgiving, feeling that if I saw no more, but were obliged to return next day to Europe, my journey would have been well repaid.

That is a mood which must come to many Holy Land pilgrim-travellers, and not always when and where they most expect it. It didn't come to Macleod, for example, in Bethlehem, even though the cave under the Church of the Nativity was one of the "holy places" which he was inclined to accept as authentic, especially after seeing that the caves and grottoes were still being used in Palestine to shelter cattle. "But in spite of all probabilities in its favour I could not associate the Incarnation with what the eye saw here." However like many a traveller since, he took delight in the situation of the town, with its vistas of terraces, fields, and mountains beyond.

Victorian Protestant visitors had one advantage over their successors in a more ecumenical age. They didn't have a guilty conscience about either the theological gap with Rome or the cultural gap between Western and Eastern Christians. They didn't try as hard as modern Western pilgrims to admire what they disliked, and did not have to protest too much (like some modern enthusiasts for pilgrimage-tours) that they could see the really holy things behind the tawdriness of many holy places, some of them dubious and others hideous. Their biblical knowledge of the history of the land ensured that they travelled reverently enough.

The intensity of their experience was also heightened by something which the modern traveller cannot hope to encounter to the same extent: the survival of ways of life and of working the land which had changed relatively little since Gospel times, despite so many political, linguistic, and religious changes. That most conspicuously helped the painters of Gospel themes, like Holman Hunt in the nineteenth century and even the immensely popular William Hole in the early part of this one, but it also enriched the experience of literary travellers like Macleod.

Sometimes, however, the Victorian travellers give the impression that they profited most from their pilgrimage when they could find solitude and even desolation. At Nazareth, for example, Macleod visited no church and avoided the rival Latin and Greek sites of the Annunciation, but after sunset left the camp, pitched in an olive-grove on the edge of the town, for a solitary and meditative walk in the surrounding hills, reflecting on a question which still arises: whether the emphasis on Christ's humanity suggested by surroundings where he walked, worked, and talked weakens the sense of his divinity. And around the Sea of Galilee, where he called the fishermen from their nets and taught and fed the crowds, the sparsity of nineteenth-century population may have made it easier for pilgrims to reflect on the mysteries of the faith as well as the once-bustling environment in which Jesus preached, healed, and went to a wedding feast. Macleod sat on the shore of the lake where the storm was stilled and thought of the simplicity and pathos of the last chapter of St John's Gospel - of the fishing and the breakfast after the Resurrection "and its exquisite harmony with all we know and believe of Jesus". He decided there was no cause for sorrow in not knowing where particular events had happened. For the truth remained, independently of the circumstances of time and place where it was first spoken.

But it is in Jerusalem that the pilgrim inevitably encounters the full range of impressions, emotions, and tensions provoked by the way Christian claims about eternity relate to events of time and place. It is usually the experience of going up to Jerusalem that completes and sums up every pilgrim's progress to the Holy Land. It is also where he may be most aware of the contrast between everyday experiences among the life of a strange city and the extraordinary things - "almost too wonderful to be", as one Christian hymn puts it - that are associated with the history of the place as well as the eschatological visions of Zion.

Norman Macleod went there after his exultant meditation on Nebi Samwil, before his excursion to Bethlehem and Hebron and the caravan's return journey through Samaria and Galilee to catch an Austrian steamer at Beirut. The dragoman had booked the party into an inn called "The Damascus" which seems to have been a cross between a traditional *khan* and a European-style hotel and whose other guests included an English party who regularly rose early, sometimes before dawn, to go to the Church of the Holy Sepulchre. The hotel had clean rooms, flagged floors, mosquito nets, and a water-pump near the party's bedroom doors. But Macleod did not know "whether there were any persons in the hotel in the capacity of host or waiters". The party's own hired retainers, who had been allotted a space where they lived much as in the desert, did the cooking in the open air and provided the room service. The muleteers seem to have bedded down in the stables.

Any pilgrim diary of Jerusalem has to mingle records of the inconsequential and encounters with the sublime. Most of us are not very succesful but Macleod produced a minor Christian masterpiece in the mixture of moods, observation, and reflections which provided the two Jerusalem instalments of *Eastward*.

The moods range from gentle reproof of a friend - who warned him that because his narrative was reaching Jerusalem he must "be very serious now and have no more jokes" - to a religious ecstasy which he managed to share and communicate. Yet we know from the unpublished letters of one of his travelling companions, William Mure of Caldwell, that Macleod was "a most capital companion in this country and very entertaining and amusing". Macleod's observations range from collecting letters at the post office, "a queer sort of cabin reached by a flight of outside stairs" near the Jaffa gate, to noting the piety of the Jews at the "place of wailing" - in contrast to the letters home of Mure, who could scarcely see beyond the abject appearance of the Jews and their "horrible cringing air to strangers". Macleod also recorded an encounter with the lepers on Mount Zion who emerged from their squalid seclusion to seek alms. His reflections, inevitably mingling with obervations, are inspired by a wide range of Jerusalem experiences - at Bishop Gobat's prayer-book service, on two visits to the Church of the Holy Sepulchre, on the Mount of Olives, and among the Muslim holy places on the Temple Mount, which had only recently become accessible to Christian pilgrims.

Earlier Christian travel-writers about Jerusalem had to rely on hearsay about the Temple Mount or had to quote accounts from a few Franks who had, by subterfuge or bribery, evaded the Muslim prohibition on "infidels". Roberts painted it from afar. Benjamin Disraeli, who found his stay in Jerusalem the most delightful week in an East Mediterranean tour, unsuccessfully tried to enter in disguise but managed to escape from the guardians and preserve his political prospects, consoled by "a glorious glimpse of splendid courts and light airy gates". In his first Jerusalem book Bartlett recorded how Frederick Catherwood, an engineer working for Mehemet Ali, got into the Haram in 1833 with two friends under cover of making a survey. In his second book some of his less gripping pages are an account of an abortive attempt to be smuggled in disguised as a Muslim woman.

But by 1864 the Haram or Temple Mount was open - at a price - to such Western visitors as Macleod. The first exceptions were made for exalted personages. The future King Leopold II of the Belgians, while Duke of Brabant, was said to have "succeeded in opening the bolted door with a golden key". When Dean Stanley revisited Palestine in 1861 in attendance on the future Edward VII he was able to visit places inaccessible to him nine years earlier and noted that even then he owed entry to the Mosque at Hebron (reputed burial place of Abraham, Isaac, and Jacob) "entirely to the privilege accorded to the Prince of Wales".

Norman Macleod was by no means the first Scot to cross the once-forbidden threshold in Jerusalem. There had been others in the early 1860's, and an unpublished journal in the National Library of Scotland records an earlier visit by a Scots doctor, J. Ivor Murray, who was allowed to visit the Mosque of Omar along with the party of "the Prince of Austria" - unnamed, but presumably the ill-fated Maximilian who was shot in Mexico. Murray was less impressed than Macleod was to be. "After all, there is not much to see. The mosk is much the same as others and were it not that it is built on the site of Solomon's Temple would deserve little notice."

Dr Murray came to Palestine from the Far East to offer his services to the Army during the Crimean War, in which Britain and France were Turkey's allies, and the war seems to have been the occasion for a permanent change of policy which was also an outward and visible symbol of the increasing Ottoman dependence on Western, and especially British, good will. By 1864, as Macleod wrote: "All, without respect of persons but only of purse, can enter it now." The fee and *baksheesh* came to about £1 a head, and there were formalities to be gone through and some difficulties surrounding them.

But the dragoman managed the formalities and the difficulties were magnified by self-interested guides and commissionaires.

The fee does not always seem to have been so high, at least for large groups. One of the more ponderous literary travellers of the time, the Rev Fergus Ferguson, a Scots Congregationalist of the Evangelical Union persuasion, was one of a party of 40 who toured the Haram the morning after he had been part of the large congregation who crowded the English church when the Prince of Wales (the future Edward VII) was there, singing "Jesus shall reign where'er the sun" to the tune of the Old Hundredth and keeping "his eyes fixed on the minister during the delivery of the greater part of his discourse."

The relative novelty of the Haram experience and the visit to the great mosques helps to explain why a substantial proportion of Macleod's description of Jerusalem is given up to the Temple Mount. He was also influenced by the undoubted authenticity of the site and by "reverential wonder" in thinking of its association, in the days of the Temple, with Christ. But he also found it congenial. He said that on entering the Mosque of Omar, as the Dome of the Rock was frequently, if not quite accurately called, "one is immediately and irresistibly struck by its exquisite proportions, its simplicity of design, and wonderful beauty. Nowhere have I seen seen stained-glass windows of such intense and glowing colours." And if he made this concession to Muslim aesthetics, he could also identify with the Old Testament in a way that some modern Christians may have forgotten and others have never learned.

> Standing here one loves to linger on earlier days and to recall the holy men and women, the kings, high priests and prophets who came to this spot to pray - whose faith is our own, whose sayings are our guide, whose life is our example, and whose songs are our hymns of worship.

But another consideration, in addition to their appreciation of Muslim variety and harmony of colour and their sense of continuity with Israel, drew mid-Victorian Protestants to the Temple Mount. Most of them disliked the gaudiness, even tawdriness, of the Church of the Holy Sepulchre - as visitors today often do, though more reticent about admitting it - and some even advanced the theory that the tomb of Christ had been on the Temple's Mount Moriah. According to this theory, mainly associated with the architectural writer James Fergusson, the great mosque was built on the site of Constantine's original Church of the Sepulchre. Macleod found it hard to accept that Joseph of Arimathea had been allowed to lay the body of Jesus in a tomb only 50 yards from the Temple wall and that the events of the Resurrection morning could have occurred so close to a heavily guarded site. But he took notice of the theory in the way that later Victorian travellers were to do with the next, and more plausible or convincing alternative tomb, that in "Gordon's Calvary", before concluding that there would be no need for lamentation if the true site were never found nor finally settled:

> We have a vision of our own -
> Ah, why should we undo it?

The problem for many pilgrims was (and is) that the sights and sounds of the traditional Church of the Holy Sepulchre, as well as the demeanour of its various and often rival custodians, seemed at odds with the vision. Bonar and McCheyne had made a visit "which awakened in our minds only feelings painful and revolting." Bartlett, who thought that early Christian tradition probably had passed on the site of the crucifixion, wrote of the way many "palpable absurdities" bred disgust and revulsion and found the history of pilgrim devotion more impressive than the church. Macleod, who spent much of his second visit to the church observing the pilgrims, had no faith in this being the true sepulchre. "Had I thought so it would only have filled me with pain and with a deeper longing to be able to lift those pilgrims up from the shadow to the substance; to remind them with the voice of a brother: He is not here, he is risen." But he found it impossible not to be moved by the ceaseless stream of pilgrims - Greeks, Russians, French, Italians, Germans and Portuguese. Some of the pilgrims, he thought, showed an expression of stolid ignorance and superstition, as if they were performing a mysterious sacred duty. But he wrote of the enthusiastic devotion of others, and especially of a woman who kissed the stone at the supposed Calvary again and again, "pressing her lips against it as if it were the dead face of her first-born."

Macleod's own experience of spiritual ecstasy was most marked on the Mount of Olives, where he wandered alone on Palm Sunday, carrying his Bible, before leaving Jerusalem for Samaria and Galilee. "It was a day never to be forgotten", he wrote, "one of those heavenly days which cannot die, but become part of one's life." He went by the Via Dolorosa to St Stephen's Gate and by Gethsemane to the slopes of the hill, looking back across the old city "until it seemd to be a dream, a white ghostly city in the silent air". He read the prophecies of Jesus about Jerusalem and realised that summer was near when he saw a fig-tree putting out its leaves, bringing home to him Jesus' words (Matthew 24.32) about when the branch "is yet tender".

There were times in Palestine, he said, when the past seemed so present and Christ and his words so living and real that he would not have been surprised if someone appeared and said: "I heard him and saw him". It was such a day.

> I wandered among the solitude of Olivet - hardly knowing where. I sat and read my Bible under one tree and then under another; descended some glen, or unknown and solitary nook, feeling only that this was Olivet and the whole hill was consecrated by the Saviour.

Then, perhaps came the real fulfilment of his pilgrimage. Thanking God for the opportunity to visit these places, he "felt if possible still more thankful for the conviction now deepened that the poorest in my parish at home... could through simple faith and childlike love enjoy the presence, the grace, and the peace of Christ, as truly as if they had been able to make a pilgrimage to the Holy Land.

"Most thankful was I for knowing that the person, not the place was holy - that his love was not local but universal." Not even on that blessed day, he said, was he tempted to think that Christ was nearer or prayer more real than among the every-day world of Glasgow.

Macleod's name is well remembered in Scotland for his good example and good works. He also deserves to have a good book rescued from obscurity. Its simplicity, its moderation, its balance, and its conviction give a valuable picture of the Palestine of his day and lasting guidance on how to profit from pilgrimage and keep it in its true Christian perspective.

# PART TWO: THE TRANSFORMATION OF PALESTINE

## 5 ECCENTRICS, SOLDIERS, AND SURVEYS

### *Spafford's colony, Wilson's map, and Gordon's Calvary*

An astonishing range of Westerners took advantage of the new opportunities to visit Palestine in the second half of the nineteenth century. Though still outnumbered by Eastern Christian visitors, among them increasing numbers of Russian peasants, their presence was beginning to change the ways of the country and even the face of the land. A smaller number of Westerners, from surveyor-soldiers and consuls to teachers and missionaries, spent longer terms in the country. Some settled there, not only an increasing number of Jews but colonies of American and German Christians and a a handful of individuals inspired by personal visions. Norman Macleod wrote not unkindly of a few Britons and Americans "possessed of a monomania for the return of the Jews" or daily watching for the Saviour's personal return, but who were on every other point "sane and sensible people". Some, however, were distinctly marked by what the world called eccentricity.

There was, for example, Jeanne Merkus, known as "the Dutch countess". She was the daughter of a governor-general of the Dutch East Indies and divorced from a Leiden professor. According to the English writer Rebecca West, Jeanne Merkus's career showed what happens to a Joan of Arc "if she is unlucky enough not to be burned". She lived in Jerusalem for 15 years and began to build a mansion variously described as a villa for the use of Christ and a home for at least some of the 144,000 redeemed souls mentioned in the vision in Revelation 7.4. But she had other enthusiasms which used up her considerable wealth before she died in poverty in Utrecht and left the mansion unfinished and subject to law-suits. She was a passionate supporter of oppressed Christians in the Ottoman Empire and went to Bosnia-Herzegovina to join a Serb rebellion, fighting with guerrillas before joining the Serb army in Belgrade and using up her money by buying the Serbs Krupp munitions. After losing possession of the house and its vast foundations she remained in Jerusalem for a time as guest in the American colony founded in 1882. Bertha Spafford Vester, daughter of its founder Horatio Spafford, remembered her as loving pretty clothes but appearing to wear top-boots under her enveloping skirts.

Spafford himself might have been counted eccentric, but his life mingled misfortune, acrimony, vision, and achievement. He had been a successful Chicago lawyer and supporter of the evangelist D.L. Moody, though his real-estate business was stricken by the great Chicago fire of 1871. His first four children were lost in an Atlantic shipwreck, though his wife was rescued unconscious from the sea, and his meditation on this suffering contributed to a quarrel in which, after renouncing doctrines of hell and eternal punishment, he was asked to leave the Presbyterian church where he was an elder. Later he and the colony became involved in a long-festering quarrel with the American missionaries in the Holy Land and with the United States consul, who was a Congregational minister.

His own account of his motive for going to Jerusalem was this: the city was where the Lord lived, suffered, and conquered. "I have lived and suffered, and wish to learn to conquer." His daughter, however, traced his passionate interest in the Holy Land back to a chance meeting in Edinburgh years before, during a business trip to Britain, with the Astronomer-Royal for Scotland, Professor Smith, who had become an enthusiast for British-Israel theories about the lost tribes and had recently completed intricate measurements of the Great Pyramid, which he thought was the "great pillar"

mentioned by Isaiah and held the key to many biblical
mysteries.

Another claim made by Spafford's daughter, however,
points to the difficulty of deciding who is to be considered
"eccentric", especially in relation to Jerusalem. Charles Gordon
- then known as "Chinese Gordon" but remembered now as
Gordon of Khartoum - took a year's sabbatical in Palestine in
1883, during which he worked out a flight-plan for Noah's
dove, the site of the Garden of Eden, and - for he was a
formidable engineer as well as a mystic - a plan to by-pass the
Suez Canal and fulfil a prophecy in Zechariah 14.8 about
living waters. His modern biographer, Charles Chenevix
Trench, describes his vision of the heavenly temple as "a kind
of celestial telephone exchange". Gordon stayed at what was
then the hill retreat of Ein Karem, though today it has the
Hebrew University medical centre on one side and the Yad
Vashem Holocaust memorial on the other. But he became
friendly with the Spaffords, often visited the colony, and
studied the landscape, opposite the north wall of the old city
and the Damascus Gate, from their flat roof. There, Bertha
Vester claims, Gordon conceived his idea that Golgotha, the
place of the skull, is a hill near the traditional Jeremiah's
Grotto which does indeed still resemble the shape of a skull.
The modern translation "dead man's head" makes a valid
point. From that identification came the theory of "Gordon's
Calvary" and the Evangelical Protestant love and care for the
holy place that modern pilgrims know as the Garden Tomb.

It looked a likely Calvary. It still does, even with an old
Muslim cemetery on top and a new station for Arab buses
down below. It was outside the city wall but not remote from
it, and it fitted in with the Roman idea that crucifixions should
be on a site visible from a main road to the city, as a reminder
and deterrent to travellers. It also looked an attractive Calvary
to those who found the Church of the Holy Sepulchre a most
unattractive as well as totally unrecognisable one.

Gordon, however, did not depend on the view from the
Spaffords' roof. He used a mixture of mystical mathematics,
intuition, intelligent guess-work, and practical research. The
area was one where a German, Otto Theunis, had already
suggested an alternative site for Calvary. Another British

officer who did surveys in Palestine, Colonel Claude Conder, had taken a similar view and thought the Church of the Holy Sepulchre "a grim and wicked old building". He too had a tomb-site.

Having placed his Golgotha, Gordon could assume that the tomb was at no great distance, since John's Gospel is explicit that the cross and the garden with the new sepulchre were close together. There was in fact a tomb close at hand, discovered in 1867: a first-century tomb which could have been in a garden, as it is today in the serene and beautiful enclave of the Garden Tomb. It was soon to be cared for by a British evangelical association among whose first trustees were the Duke of Argyll and the Earl of Aberdeen. Its enthusiastic advocates included Sir Henry Rider Haggard, now best remembered as author of *King Solomon's Mines*. "Who can tell whether or no it is the very spot?", he wrote. "At least the sight of it is a great support to the imagination. Such a garden there must have been, and such a tomb, even as we see them today." Another visitor who was all but convinced (on an 1892 visit) was Dr James Robertson, minister of Whittingehame in East Lothian, where his parishioners included a rising young Conservative politician, able and well connected with the English Cecils, called Arthur Balfour. The sight of the tomb stirred "the profoundest feeling" in Robertson when he thought of the Resurrection morning. He could not be sure but reflected: "The impression is hardly less when we say to ourselves: if not here, in just such a place, and possibly in a spot very little removed from this."

Some Christians believe the Garden Tomb is the authentic site. Some of us hope it is, or wish it were. Those who visit it will be grateful to Gordon, whatever they think of his celestial mathematics.

There are other Victorian soldiers who passed that way who mingled with the pilgrims, who were often pilgrims themselves, and to whom subsequent visitors and residents have good cause to be grateful. One of them was Conder, a soldier of prodigious scholarly attainments who guided the future George V on a Holy Land tour in 1882 as Arthur Stanley had done for his father. Conder had earlier been sent out along with another young officer of the Royal Engineers, the future Lord Kitchener, to undertake surveys under an arrangement between the Palestine Exploration Fund and the War Office which shows the extent to which the Turkish Government had now to conform to Western and especially British wishes.

Kitchener surveyed east of the Jordan and in Galilee. Conder, who hoped East European Jews would come to develop the land, mapped out much of Palestine, identified biblical sites, and traced the course of migrations and wars.

The two other oustanding military surveyors were Charles Wilson and Charles Warren, both later knighted. Warren, also an enthusiast for Jewish settlement and even Jewish government of Palestine, was to have a chequered career after leaving Palestine. As Metropolitan Police Commissioner he was blamed for mishandling the "Bloody Sunday" riots in Trafalgar Square in 1887. As a Boer War general he contributed to mismanagement at Spion Kop. Later he backed Baden-Powell in setting up the Scout movement. But he took a major part in the first extensive scientific excavation to reveal layers of history buried under Jerusalem and made significant reports on the potential for agricultural and economic revival in Palestine. The Royal Engineers were doing work which today would be handled by archaeologists and economic consultants. In Palestine Warren's public relations were better than in his police service, and he seems to have been long-suffering with clerical visitors. For example the Revd Andrew Thomson of Broughton Place in Edinburgh - author of the phrase about the "desire and dream of a lifetime" and one of the better books of clerical travels - was allowed into Warren's workings. He left a valuable description of the British engineers at work, together with hints of the reluctance of Turkish co-operation and the resentment of the Muslim religious leaders looking down from the Haram.

Wilson, however, is better remembered in modern Jerusalem, partly because his name was given to "Wilson's Arch", close to the Western Wall, which carries the main road from the Old City to the Temple Mount. He was later to be involved in the belated bid to rescue Gordon from Khartoum and took a leading part in the Palestine Exploration Fund and its literary off-shoot, the Palestine Pilgrim Text Society. The reports of the P.E.F. were to record Wilson's enthusiasm for Jewish colonisation and his observation of the way that, even before the end of the century, it was changing the hitherto desolate face of many parts of the land.

It is to Charles Wilson that we mainly owe the Ordnance Survey map of 1864-65 (scale 1:2500) which enables us to see the pattern of streets and buildings which the Victorian pilgrims encountered. A glance at it makes plain what many words might fail to convey: for example the extent to which Jerusalem was dominated by the Haram as it had once been by the Temple, and the pathetically small scale of the Wailing Wall or Place of Wailing, which appears on Wilson's map as no more than a tiny alleyway, but which was (and is) sacred to the Jews as both a remnant of the Temple and the symbol for their lamentation of its destruction. All Christian travellers seem to have visited it, though not all noted (as Edward Jonas did) that Moslem rulers received "an exorbitant sum of money for the privilege" which allowed the Jews access to pray at the place.

In addition to these military surveyors, Victorian Palestine had even a maritime survey of sorts by the evangelical canoeist John MacGregor, author of *The Rob Roy on the Jordan*. Himself nicknamed Rob Roy, he also gave the name to a succession of canoes on which he paddled the Baltic and the Danube as well as the Waters of Damascus, the Sea of Galilee, and as much of the Jordan as proved navigable.

Despite his Scottish ancestry, MacGregor was a man of the Temple - the lawyers' one in London and not the holy one in Jerusalem. His great enthusiasms were sailing and evangelism, especially the London Open-Air Mission which he founded. In Syria and Palestine he was more an observer than a missionary when not preoccupied with "waltzing" in his canoe or supervising its overland carriage on horseback on a pole frame. However his religious reflections often have a freshness missing from those of many visiting clergymen.

His trip brought troubles of the kind that dragomans were hired to prevent, but MacGregor's dragoman and baggage proceeded separately by land. Near Lake Huleh in Northern Galilee, an area much drained by later Jewish settlers and now a country of showpiece *kibbutzim*, he was taken prisoner by local Arabs who formed a line across the river and lifted the canoe (with MacGregor still in it) to the local sheikh's tent. He eventually had to pay ransom but reflected that it was his own fault, as the Eastern traveller should either have arranged adequate protection from the ruling power or contracted with the local sheikh for protection. He also reckoned that the Huleh Arabs, far from centres of Eastern commerce, let him go for far less than the going rate: he paid a gold napoleon (slightly smaller than a sovereign) but thought an Englishman was really worth £100.

After sailing on calmer waters on the Sea of Galilee MacGregor denounced the filthy town of Tiberias, especially its Jewish quarter, but complained that the Jews didn't ask for "what the world would give them free, their own beloved Palestine". He mingled denunciations of unkempt rabbis with a list of admirable Jewish qualities remarkable in the nineteenth century for the inclusion of "military prowess" along with learning, science, and musical talent.

He also had strong views on another nation making its presence felt in Palestine. Although some of the best oriental travellers were Americans - he instanced W.M. Thomson of Beirut and Professor Robinson - "these cousins of ours do their sight-seeing so uncommon quick". MacGregor met about 30 Americans and complained that they made the mistake of going to too many places rather than seeing some of them well. "Above all the East must be seen deliberately." He almost got round to saying: "If it's Tuesday it must be Nazareth". His observations are roughly contemporary with Mark Twain's American humour at the expense of Americans in *The Innocents Abroad*, but the great American humourist was too sceptical and superficial to write much of value about Palestine.

A "surveyor" of a different sort who carefully avoided being uncommon quick, but was a lover and benefactor of the Holy Land, was Canon H.B. Tristram. He almost became Bishop in Jerusalem in succession to Gobat. Shaftesbury urged him strongly on Disraeli. The Premier was willing but the Anglo-Prussian scheme was doomed, Tristram declined, and the chance passed. Instead Tristram is remembered best for his careful observation, surveying, and recording of the birds, animals, flowers, plants, trees and fish of Palestine and of areas which are now in Jordan, Lebanon, or Syria. His studies covered geology as well as natural history.

Wilson, Warren, and Conder showed how human application could help revive the Holy Land. Tristram rejoiced in its natural phenomena, as he found them and as they were recorded in the Bible. He was also a Christian environmentalist before the word was thought of. The Holy Land, he said, not only elucidates but bears witness to the truth of the Holy Book.

But Tristram's *The Land of Israel*, his record of journeys lasting nearly ten months in 1863-64, is also a very great travel-book and a valuable historical source. It includes one of the finest Victorian descriptions of the "gorgeous and almost dazzling" Dome of the Rock in the Haram, where he was also delighted to find a chink in the walls on which the sparrow had built a nest, and of the flowers and shrubs which still created "the excellency of Carmel". But there are harrowing descriptions of civil strife in Lebanon involving Maronites, Druse, and Muslims and the aftermath of the Syrian massacres of Christians. There are also points which history has given more significance than they seemed to have at the time. At Tiberias, for example, he noted that the Polish immigrants seemed better disposed to listen to Christian missionaries than "the native Jews", and added that children joined in mocking and jeering, crying: "This is our land, and shall be ours again. Why should Christians defile it?"

Some of Tristram's value, however, derives from the extent to which he went off the beaten track and (with some hazard, much difficulty, and considerable expenditure) went beyond the area which the Turks controlled after a fashion and where the Western consuls could exert influence. This was the time at which, as Lord Eustace Cecil (Arthur Balfour's uncle) told a reminiscent Palestine Exploration Fund meeting some years later, a man could not go beyond Jericho without being robbed and forced to return to Jerusalem "clothed in pages of the The Times newspaper". Much of Tristram's work was in the basin of the Dead Sea, and involved a well-recorded visit to the mountain fortress of Masada, scene of a forlorn Jewish stand against the Romans, which has a major part in

tourist itineraries of modern Israel but was often ignored in
earlier guides and travel-books. Those who had visited it, said
Tristram, made the ascent seem much more difficult than it
really was: "An English lady could accomplish it easily."

Agnes Smith was really an Anglo-Scottish lady rather than
an English one. She was brought up in Ayrshire but spent
most of her life in England, where she married an Anglican
clergyman who was a fellow of Corpus Christi College,
Cambridge. She endowed the English Presbyterian College
and co-operated with her twin sister Maggie in a range of
scholarly achievements, though she also wrote novels. She
was best known (as Agnes Smith Lewis) for her work on the
manuscripts in the convent of St Catherine in Sinai, where in
1893 the sisters discovered an early Syriac version of the
Gospels being used as butter dishes on the refectory table. But
her first visit to the Middle East had been in 1868-69, when the
two sisters and a teacher called Grace Blyth from their
Kensington finishing school had done a grand tour of Europe,
Egypt, and the Holy Land.

*Eastern Pilgrims* was Agnes Smith's first book and it has a
youthful freshness, almost a naiveté, that gives no hint of her
later formidable and scholarly approach. The two sisters even
parked their Kensington teacher in Jerusalem and ventured
well beyond on their own to the Jordan valley, the Dead Sea,
and Mar Saba. There they lunched in the shade of Ida Pfeiffer's
tower while some monks gazed at them from the monastery
roof. "Admission was out of the question", though the horses
and mules were allowed in to drink. "Strange hospitality",
wrote Agnes. Their dragoman tactfully delayed the news that
two Arab travellers had been murdered and others wounded
or kidnapped on their route just a day before.

The young ladies also ventured into areas where male
pilgrims were not allowed to tread. A friendly Italian doctor
in Jerusalem secured them admission to two harems. One,
within the Haram, was that of the senior of the three wives of
the Mufti of Jerusalem, who (as Agnes delicately put it) "had
the honour of lodging him by turns". Much of the visit was
devoted to an inspection of dresses, but the visitors were
introduced to one of the junior wives and heard the Mufti's ten
year-old son read from the Koran. They were offered lemon-

ade, which they presumably accepted, and narghilehs - Eastern "hubble-bubble" water-pipes or hookahs - which they presumably declined.

On such rounds they gathered some footnotes for the cultural and social history of Victorian Jerusalem - for example that there was only one pianoforte in the city - and some curious snippets of conversation. However distorted in translation and recollection, they reveal something of the confusion which the Western presence had brought to the the the Ottoman Empire in decline. For example the Mufti's chief wife told her visitors "that she wished to be civilised". Agnes also recorded that Turks and Jews would not give British Protestants the title of Christians, but intended that denial as a compliment. "You do not worship images, nor kiss the sepulchre, nor cross yourselves. You must be Mohammedans of another sect. We think too highly of you to give you such an insulting name."

Agnes Smith, who reported local criticisms of missionary zeal for conversions, also noted the respect in which the German Kaiserswerth deaconesses were held in Jerusalem. But she remained realist enough to add that "European ladies cannot walk unattended in the streets". Some did, however, take Norman Macleod's advice that "a strong lady may accompany her husband".

Among such couples were the Pitts from Mitcham in Surrey. George Pitt was a retired Quaker draper who rejected the phrase "Holy Land" as superstitious and declined to use the pagan names of months. He was also as compulsive a traveller as Ida Pfeiffer nearly 40 years before - and, like her, determined to travel as far as possible for as little as possible. Partially deaf and slow of speech, he depended on his wife to be his "ear and mouthpiece", he said. "I discovered she had a travelling talent and did not like to wrap it up."

Despite his disability, Pitt wrapped up various travels in Europe, America, the Middle East, and round the world via China and Japan for a Quaker magazine called *The British Friend*, and although extremely economical for a Victorian with his words and descriptive passages, included some detail that loftier travellers disdained. He and his wife both wore drab Cheviot suits "and needed no change of outer garments".

They travelled light, with a Gladstone bag and a large palm-
leaf basket. Among the basket's contents were a kettle and a
portable spirit-lamp, which served as a mini-stove for boiling
eggs as well as making tea in their bedrooms.

As a result their journey to Palestine - out via Hamburg,
back via Venice and Paris - cost them only a third of what
other travellers paid, even though they incurred the cost of a
dragoman, horses, and servants once they reached Jerusalem.
They dealt through Howard's Hotel, whose owner they
described as "the great rival of T. Cook the London excursion-
ist", paying half the cost in advance and half on completion of
the Palestine trip. They got favourable terms as the autumn
was "a slack time". Another of their economies had been to
travel up from Jaffa on the new van that starting bumping
along at 4pm, "travelling overnight for coolness". The other
passengers were three Arabs carrying swords, guns, daggers,
and pistols. The whole trip lasted 108 days, of which 27 were
in Palestine, 20 of them on horseback. The cost averaged "11
shillings a day each, including all fares, fees, board, lodging,
gratuities, guides, postage, and every conceivable expense save
presents for home." Of this 6s11d, (a good draper's price) went
on travel, at just over a penny a mile. The total cost worked
out at under £60 a head.

A cheap Victorian cruise worked out at about a guinea a
day, plus extras, and some years after the Pitts' trip there was
a Lunn-Perowne 21 day cruise via Marseilles on offer at 21
guineas. It touched Palestine, if only just, and a scramble up to
Jerusalem would (like other excursions) be extra.

The Pitts' pilgrimage on a tight budget was in 1881. It was
to be a more momentous year for Palestine than they realised,
and one whose events soon brought changes far more dramatic than the van that linked Jaffa and Jerusalem. Early in the
year the relatively liberal Tsar Alexander II had been murdered in St Petersburg. His death ushered in a new and bitter
era of repression in Russia, one symptom of which was a fresh
wave of anti-Semitism and semi-official incitement of persecution of Jews, even pogroms. When the Pitts toured Russia less
than two years after their return from the Holy Land they
noted, as all travellers did, the size of the Jewish population of
Russian Poland. The reaction and persecution which marked

1881 were followed by what Zionism calls the first wave or ascent of the modern Jewish settlement - or resettlement - of Palestine, now conventionally dated in 1882.

It was already clear then that Palestine was changing dramatically, and obvious that the feeble Turkish grip on the province was likely to be further weakened. These distant events in Russia were to play a vital part in determining some of the patterns of change. Influences on the Holy Land were increasingly to involve settlers as well as surveyors, pilgrims, and tourists. The steamers from the Black Sea were bringing increased numbers of Russian peasants for whom an Easter in Jerusalem was the desire and dream of a lifetime. A different desire, and another kind of dream, influenced Jews from the Russian Empire. There had always been some coming to the Holy Land to pray and to die. A handful at first, but a significant handful, were coming to build a new kind of life in Palestine.

# 6  THE SCRAMBLE FOR PALESTINE

## *ZIONIST PIONEERING AND ARAB AWAKENING*

The years from the 1880's to the First World War were an interlude of progress and peace in Palestine. There was a relative calm before the great storms that were to come, even though it was rippled by contradictions and overshadowed by long-term uncertainties. What happened then shaped much of what the pilgrim and tourist encounter today.

Versions of the Holy Land's history in these years can be presented from different standpoints. All are important and none tells the whole truth. All are liable to be told, whether consciously or not, with benefit of hindsight and under the influence of later events which delight or depress the historians.

The Israeli heirs of Zionism emphasise the creation of Jewish agricultural colonies, the development of modern Hebrew, the spread of Jerusalem as a mainly Jewish city far beyond its ancient walls, and the foundation of Tel Aviv on the sandy wastes up the coast from Jaffa.

Palestinian Arabs and their sympathisers trace the first stirrings of Arab nationalism, at this stage a protest against Turkish rule rather than Western influence and most evident among those, including local Christians, influenced by Western education and ideas. These were stirrings of Arab consciousness, however, rather than of any sense of Palestinian nationality. The Turkish Empire did not include a distinct province of Palestine, which was traditionally seen as part of Syria; and, though from 1888 there was a Sanjak of Jerusalem, this excluded Samaria and Galilee. The modern English Roman Catholic historian Christopher Sykes calls Turkish Palestine not a country but a hotch-potch. The great Scots scholar George Adam Smith described it as a "land of tribes" - both historically and when he encountered it in the 1880's. He seemed to imply it always would be.

But diplomatic historians might depict a scramble for Palestine among the Great Powers - seemlier and statelier than the "scramble for Africa" but certainly a scramble for influence and an anxiety to prepare for the probable contingency of Turkish collapse. Sir Charles Wilson, the great surveyor, spoke in 1899 of a "scramble for holy places", deploring the bad taste of many of the new buildings set on them and the damage done to archaeological remains. But the Turks themselves had a hand in the game, skilful in playing on the rivalries of the Great Powers and eager by fits and starts to modernise their empire. They exploited these rivalries to hang on to parts of the empire in the Balkans and, but for the First World War, might have survived much longer in Palestine. The European powers managed to be at odds and in concert at the same time, like the various Christian Churches. Their influence, generally and individually, ensured that there was nothing comparable to the chronic conflict in such Turkish provinces as Macedonia and no cruel persecution to compare with that of the Armenians, who were consistently oppressed and intermittently massacred with the connivance of the Turkish Government and the eager co-operation of the Kurds. The Turks had one rule for the Levant coast and another for the distant hills, far from the pilgrim trade and the consuls.

There are no reliable population statistics for Turkish Palestine in its last phase. By modern standards it was certainly sparse, though it had probably doubled in the second half of the nineteenth century. In 1885 the entire population of Syria, the Lebanon, Palestine and what is now Jordan was estimated at 2,185,000. Modern Israeli estimates put the population of Palestine at not much more than 500,000 at the turn of the century, less than 10% of 1990 estimates.

It is possible to be less imprecise about the growth of the Jewish minority and to be relatively definite about Jerusalem, where that minority had become a local majority somewhere between 1865 and 1880. In 1880, before the first modern wave of settlement, the total Jewish population of Palestine may have been 15,000, not much more than in the days of Bonar and McCheyne. It had grown by 1914 to about 85,000, still well under a fifth of the population.

Jerusalem grew from a small city of about 15,000 people in the mid-1860s to 70,000 in 1912, of whom 45,000 were Jewish, and the remainder (excluding foreigners) divided between Christian and Muslim Arabs. Robert Black, a Scots layman from Peebles who had been in Jerusalem in 1879, returned in 1895 to note that the city was "much improved since my last visit. The streets are better paved ... The town is swarming with English travellers and tourists." The expanding population, and the tourist or pilgrim trade which was its major industry, could no longer be confined within the historic Jewish, Christian, and Muslim quarters of the Old City. Nor did it feel driven there by fear of marauders. New colonies or "quarters" were built. The largest group of them, mainly Jewish, on the bare hills west of Jerusalem gradually merged into a new city. Its new Jewish quarters were separated from the walls by an area where population was mixed and where a modern commercial centre began to emerge. New hotels were built for tourists in this area, as well as new hospices for poorer pilgrims. There was a German Catholic hospice outside the Damascus Gate, a large French one some way along the walls from it, and a Russian one on what became a prime site a bit down the Jaffa Road, as well as on the Mount of Olives. The Franciscans at the Casa Nuova began to emphasise a rule that pilgrims could stay free for ten days - with gifts welcome - provided their "rite" offered no similar facilities in Jerusalem.

Religion was inseparable from politics and diplomacy in the Holy Land, but the European and Christian denominational rivalries were often reflected in good works as well as new churches, including the St George's north of the walls which became the Anglican cathedral. Many of the landmarks of the Old City of Jerusalem and the Mount of Olives, which modern visitors contrast with the new Israeli city, date only from this relatively modern period, when the Churches (and the parallel Jewish efforts) also gave Palestine some of the public services of a modern society. In the 1880s a German leper hospital and a British opthalmic hospital were built on the Bethlehem side of Jerusalem; there were also schools, orphanages, and hospitals sponsored by the Churches and missionary societies, not only in Jerusalem but all around the Holy Land.

There was now a substantial and complex missionary presence in Palestine and adjacent parts of Syria and Lebanon. The most significant educational and cultural influence was probably that of the Americans in Beirut. In Palestine itself the emphasis in Anglican and Lutheran activities had spread from Jewish missions to more general educational and social work which helped to build up local Churches whose congregations tended be drawn from the existing Arab Christian communities. The Church Missionary Society had probably now more influence on the course of Palestinian history than the Church Missions to Jews.

Even the Scottish missionary activities had become very diversified. The Edinburgh Medical Missionary Society had founded the hospital which still serves Nazareth today and also worked in Damascus. From 1884 the Free Church of Scotland had a mission led by the formidable Dr David Watt Torrance at Tiberias on the Sea of Galilee and later extended its work to Safed. Although its most conspicuous achievement was the Tiberias hospital opened in 1894, it also had an influence in education and made some converts. Later the United Free Church (as it had become) also took over a medical mission in Hebron. The "Established" section of Scots Presbyterianism had its main mission in the region at Beirut but also found itself backing the Tabeetha School (with associated medical work) set up in Jaffa by Miss Jane Walker Arnott of Edinburgh - described in its earlier days by the visiting American writer Charles Dudley Warner as one of several missions "conducted as private enterprises by ladies of culture". He found that most of the pupils were daughters of local Christian families, taught in Arabic but learning to sing English words and tunes. He also understated the mixture of faith, zeal, and skill with which Miss Arnott and the other ladies of culture overcame private prejudice and official obstruction - and developed marketing techniques to attract the attention of visiting American writers and other potential benefactors. Among them was the leader of what the school visitors' book records as Mr Cook's Palestinian Tour. Thomas

Cook of "London and Leicester" is the last of that party's 21 signatories.

As well as missionaries came tourists, pilgrims, philanthropists, royal princes, artists, writers, scholars, dreamers, and schemers, such as the Christian Zionist Laurence Oliphant, journalist and sometime M.P., who tried to persuade the Turks to let Jewish settlers develop the "Eastern Palestine" which we now call Jordan. To list and quote them all would be beyond the scope of any but the most specialised and scholarly work but there are a few who should be mentioned for their own intrinsic interest or their role in history. Among them are such very different personalities as Sir George Adam Smith, Elizabeth Butler, the German Kaiser Wilhelm II, and the Viennese journalist and dramatist Theodor Herzl.

Smith was a Scots Free Church college professor who later became Principal of Aberdeen University and also found himself advising the British Foreign Office during the First World War. He was a Hebrew scholar, biblical expert, and ancient historian (knighted in 1916) who wrote one of the great books about Palestine, *The Historical Geography of the Holy Land*. When it appeared in 1894, drawing on work that Smith had begun on his first visit to Palestine in 1880, it displaced Dean Stanley's *Sinai and Palestine* from its pre-eminence - partly because, as Smith argued in his preface, the "recent progress of biblical criticism" (some of which Smith had encountered in post-graduate days at Leipzig and Tübingen) had wholly altered the approach of Old Testament science and scholarship since Stanley's time. Moreover, although Smith was a theologian and historian, he had an appreciation of the rising science of archaeology. "We have run most of the questions to earth", he said. "It only remains for us to dig them up."

But Smith was also a very fine writer and a great preacher in print. His descriptions of the hill-country and the wilderness of Judea, for example, and his relation of the landscape to the teachings of Christ and of Old Testament prophets, match anything in the English literature of the Holy Land. There has never been a more powerful sermon on Jesus as the Good Shepherd than in Smith's description of the shepherds of Judea. Its basis was observation in the hills - watching several shepherds come down to a well to let their flocks mingle. Yet they were easily disentangled, for the sheep knew the voices and would not follow a stranger. You understand the role of the shepherd of Judea in the Old Testament and in Gospel teaching, said Smith, when you meet him, sleepless, far-sighted, weather-beaten, "and looking out over his scattered sheep, every one of them on his heart".

Smith's papers in the National Library of Scotland reveal the scale of operations still demanded even of a college professor who ventured beyond the tourist pale of Jerusalem and Bethlehem towards Hebron or into these Judean hills. An escort "with sword, pistols, and musket" was still needed - this was on a 1901 visit - and the party mustered 32 animals (13 horses, 15 mules, four asses) and seven tents. There were Hanna the dragoman, whom Smith has specially asked for after good service on an earlier trip, Francis and another camp waiter, Yusuf the lunch waiter, Iskander the cook and his assistant, together with various grooms and muleteers.

"You can imagine the crowd", he wrote home to his wife, assuring her that he had hot-water bottles put in at 9.45 - all part of the Cook's service. But in Jerusalem he had found the water only fit for hot water-bottles. "The only thing I have anxiety about is the want of water and the evil and stagnant nature of what remains ....We dare not touch the Jerusalem water, which is very bad, so we drink Appolinaris and Rishon-le-Zion wine." Smith's son Lord Balerno told me in the 1980's that his father had begun with the temperance enthusiasm then growing in his part of the Kirk but had allowed his view to be modified when prescribed wine while recovering from a bout of typhus. Rishon-le-Zion, ("first in Zion") was one of the early Jewish settlements. Its wine was later to commend itself also to Winston Churchill.

Reckless or pious pilgrims and travellers who drank the local water still did so at their peril. One eminent victim (in 1896) was the Austrian Archduke Karl Ludwig, brother of the Emperor Franz Josef and father of the Franz Ferdinand murdered at Sarajevo. He died from an attack of typhoid attributed to drinking water from the holy and heavily polluted River Jordan.

There was progress. One sign of the times was that on
Smith's first visit after the French-owned railway from Jaffa
reached Jerusalem in 1892 he was offered special terms by
Thomas Cook. He could have a special train, provided he had
- or would pay fares for - 60 first-class passengers at 12 guineas
each. But although most of the travellers to Palestine welcomed the signs of progress a few lamented them. One of the
more picturesque complainers was Lady Butler, an artist
whose pictures of the Palestinian landscape (used as illustra-
tions for her *Letters from the Holy Land* in 1903) are in total
contrast to those which made her famous.

Elizabeth Butler was an English Roman Catholic married
to an Irish one, Sir William Butler, a soldier whose Liberal-
Nationalist inclinations forced him from command in South
Africa on the eve of the Boer War, when he fell out of
sympathy with Milner's policy. Though she illustrated the
first book of poems by her sister, Alice Meynell, Elizabeth
Butler won fame as an artist with pictures on spectacular
military themes including "The Roll Call", "Balaklava", and
"Scotland for Ever". Her view of Palestine in spring was very
different, with Nazareth still pale in early morning sunlight
and nothing garish even in the noonday of Gethsemane. Only
one camp picture, with horses and flags and servants that look
like Arab dragoons, hints at her other artistic life.

She made the Holy Land seem more placid than it was to
be in the new century ahead. Not many Westerners before or
since would have cried: "Exquisite Nablus, what a paradise to
rest in!" Her worst fear, in this interlude of relative security,
was a false alarm that the nearest Lutheran minister was
coming to pay a courtesy call at her tent. But for all her
aversion to Protestantism she struck a mood that had its
affinities with Paul Kruger's forlorn Calvinist defence of the
old Boer lifestyle. She feared that a "Christian" Power - Britain
and Germany are meant - would allow greedy syndicates to
run factories, mines, and new towns. She found it "a strange
paradox but a very weighty fact" that Turkish rule preserved
tokens of the past for the elucidation of the Christian's Bible
but she feared that "the service of Mammon would soon
necessitate the obliteration of these tokens so precious to our
faith."

She hankered after the "vain dream" that the Holy Land might be purchased as a perpetual possession for Christendom by "some great confederation of earnest people whose god is not the dollar".

There was a similar romanticism, though from a more pro-Muslim viewpoint, in the way the French sailor and novelist Pierre Loti wrote contrasting the banality of a Jerusalem tourist hotel's commonplace drawing room and souvenir-sellers with the dark town, the old Saracen gate, and the caravanserais on the road, "citadels to shelter travellers and their mounts against robbers". But some of the most remarkable things in Palestine were happening in the countryside. Sir Charles Wilson contrasted the state of the upper Jordan valley in Galilee in 1882, when there was scarcely a trace of cultivation, with the waving masses of corn and the almond or olive trees at the end of the century. In Jewish colonies supported by Baron Edmond de Rothschild, he said, it was possible to "see what the country might become under a proper system of cultivation and probably was before the Arab conquest". He challenged the traditional view that Jews did not take kindly to agriculture and reported seeing Jewish colonists working in the fields "as if their hearts were really in their work". He also argued that the Jewish example was also beginning to change Arab agriculture.

What was significant in these, and many other people's varied thoughts on the future of Palestine, was the assumption of the vulnerability and impermanence of Turkish rule, which despite changes in the country remained both corrupt and inefficient. Many of the legal obstacles, for example, which ought to have hindered Jewish settlement and acquisition of land could be eased in practice by inducements and bribery at various levels of government - so much so that the first signs of native Arab consciousness began to emerge before there was any significant nationalist movement. In 1891 Jerusalem "notables" led a protest with 550 supporters against Jews who were said to be depriving Arabs of land, bringing in arms, and taking over local trade.

The changes were obvious, even when their ultimate direction was still unclear. When Jews acquired land it was usually by buying it from Arabs. If there were legal difficulties they were evaded by the use of ingenuity or by traditional methods of the Middle East. When Jews developed land, however, they sometimes employed Arabs - so much so that some Israeli historians raise the possibility that, but for later waves of determined Zionists, the Jewish colonists would have became a class of managers and entrepreneurs. There were also signs of friction around Jewish settlements, though it is hard there to distinguish incipient political protest from traditional marauding, and in the towns. In Jerusalem, for example, Nahum Levison, a rabbi's son from Safed who later became a Christian minister, found a contrast from his quiet native town where the streets were safe at night. In Jerusalem, where he went to a Jewish college, an escort was needed on the way to and from evening classes, and even that did not deter Arab stone-throwers. In the early years of the twentieth century friction extended from Jerusalem to Jaffa and Haifa. There was anti-Jewish feeling in the newly established Arab newspapers and ill-feeling had developed even near Levison's home in Galilee, where a Jewish land company had bought much of the land around Tiberias.

At the turn of the century there was another significant complication in the uncertainties of Palestine. British influence over the Turks was now rivalled and in some ways supplanted by the German influence (and interest in the "Berlin to Baghdad" railway) which was spectacularly demonstrated and symbolised in the Kaiser's visit to Constantinople and Jerusalem in 1898.

Wilhelm II was to be guest of honour at the opening of the new German Church of the Redeemer in the Mauristan part of Jerusalem, close to the Church of the Holy Sepulchre. But the Turks were determined to put on a display for their visitor, who wanted to ensure he put on one of his own. The city wall was breached at the Jaffa Gate to allow the Kaiser a spectacular entrance as a pilgrim-in-state. The Turkish police rounded up beggars and despatched them to country villages for the duration of the imperial visit. Even Jerusalem's stray dogs were said to have been gathered in and caged for the occasion.

The visit was the chance for Turkish officialdom to tackle work for which there was normally neither money nor enthusiasm. There was painting and plastering on the Temple

Mount and the Aksa Mosque was given a gilded look. The shed-like extensions of shops were demolished and "lamps burned all night" on the Jaffa Road. Attempts were made to bring some of Palestine's few roads up to European standards so that "carriages could safely pass". Decayed bridges were restored on the road to Haifa and the telegraph was extended to Jericho, though the Kaiser didn't go there and local Bedouin interrupted communications, acquiring useful wire rather than demonstrating for a cause. The police arrested thirty.

It was to seek advantage from this occasion that Theodor Herzl took the Orient Express to Constantinople. This gifted, intense Viennese writer had already been converted to Zionism under the influence of the French anti-Semitism revealed by the Dreyfus case. He was persuaded that Jews could only find security and be at ease in a Jewish State - a doctrine which did not convince the integrated Jews of Western Europe but matched the convictions of the poorer and persecuted Jews of the Russian Empire. He gave leadership, inspiration, and some useful connections to their aspirations; he was ready to speak politely to anyone who might help his cause, whether the Pope, the Sultan, or the Russian Government; and, though he was not quite the founder of Zionism that he is sometimes thought to be, he was its most articulate and formidable prophet. Like many other people, he saw that the Turkish decline might open the way for a Jewish State of some sort in Palestine.

In 1898 his hopes turned to the Kaiser, whose influence with the Turks had so obviously increased. He knew that the Kaiser was not unsympathetic, having already been sounded out by the Grand Duke of Baden, a supporter of Jewish colonisation. Wilhelm replied in a curious but characteristically excited letter which ranged from a theological comment on alleged Jewish responsibility for the death of Christ to anxiety about the way the "most hideous and vulgar anti-Semitism" was raising its "gruesome head". He was ready to be the protector of the Jews and thought "it would be an enormous gain for Germany if the country of the Hebrews looked to it with gratitude".

Left to himself Wilhelm would have taken up the Zionist case with the Sultan. He gave Herzl an hour's audience in

Constantinople and convinced himself that encouragement of
Jewish colonies in Palestine was in the mutual interest of
Germany and Turkey. But the German Foreign Office -
which frequently worried about imperial indiscretions - saw
matters differently and thought that encouragement of Jewish
hopes for a special status in Palestine could complicate German hopes for a Turkish alliance. Herzl took ship for Jaffa to
be at hand during the Palestinian part of the Kaiser's tour.

There he had two more meetings with the Kaiser. The first
was by the roadside near Mikveh Israel ("Hope of Israel"),
where the first Jewish agricultural school in the Holy Land
had been founded in 1870. Herzl stood bareheaded in the
Kaiser's honour while Jewish schoolchildren sang the German imperial anthem, and Wilhelm - who with all his faults
had the style of imperial majesty - rode up to Herzl, shook his
hand, and engaged him in warm and friendly conversation.
Herzl's stock soared and hopes rose, only to sink again after
the second Palestinian meeting in the Kaiser's tent, pitched
outside the walls of Jerusalem. For a formal audience it was
friendly enough. But the Kaiser's entourage had ensured that
the encouraging exchanges about colonisation and the prospects for water-power from the Jordan stopped short of any
commitment. The communiqué toned down Wilhelm's be-
nevolence and the opportunity was missed. The chance to
create a Jewish national home as a German protectorate passed
for ever.

In a few years Herzl was dead and Zionism, always
quarrelsome within itself, had been temporarily riven by the
argument over whether to pursue, even as an interim stage, an
offer by the British Colonial Secretary, Joseph Chamberlain,
to provide land for Jewish settlement in Africa. That earnest
but sketchy scheme is usually referred to as the offer of
Uganda, but had anything come of it the Jewish colonies
would probably have been on what were later, for a time,
known as the White Highlands of Kenya. Zionism, however,
was to keep its eyes fixed on Palestine, where a new wave of
Russian perseution had ensured a steady flow of Jewish
immigrants; and its next outstanding international leader, the
Russian-born Chaim Weizmann, was far more drawn to
Britain than to Germany.

Meanwhile it seemed possible that events in Turkey might dramatically change the outlook for Palestine. Between 1908 and 1914 the Turkish Empire, for long a theocratic tyranny in decay, experienced a series of political convulsions which gave the phrase "Young Turks" to the English language. Turkey began to use the language and forms of parliamentary democracy, without much substance, and encountered new waves of nationalism. The most obvious were in the Balkans, where the Turks were soon to lose their last foothold in Europe except for Eastern Thrace, but others affected the Arabic-speaking and mainly Muslim parts of the empire.

In the long run the result was the creation of a nationalist Turkey, much diminished in size, the end of the caliphate, and the emergence of the various Arab States - and Israel. But in 1908-09 there were hopes of a very different outcome, even one in which there was power-sharing and amity among Turks, Muslim Arabs, Christians, and Jews. The Jews also hoped that the new régime would help open up Palestine to them. From Tiberias the Scots medical missionary D.W. Torrance wrote home of "a modern miracle, the work of God". There was to be "freedom of speech, freedom of the press, religious freedom. The very thought of such things a year ago seemed impossible." In the squares of Tiberias he saw Muslims dancing with Jews and Christians.

But Torrance had misgivings which were soon well justified. The old order had crumbled but it was succeeded by unrest, war, and conscription for a series of wars.

There had also been rejoicing in cities bigger than Tiberias, with talk in Syria of an Arab-Turkish dual monarchy on Austro-Hungarian lines. One of the results of the revolution had been to bring above ground almost the first tender shoots of Arab nationalism, though in Mesopotamia Arab officers of the Turkish army took advantage of the new mood in a different way by forming secret societies. In distant desert Arabia Hussein ibn Ali was allowed back as Grand Sherif of Mecca, with fateful results a few years later during the Arab Revolt and the First World War.

Arab Palestinians and their sympathisers trace their nationalist tradition back to the mid-nineteenth century and the foundation of political and cultural journals, and the Syrian

Scientific Society. They quote a French traveller, Denis de Revoyre, who in 1884 reported "an Arab movement, lately risen" and a general hatred of the Turk throughout the Arab lands. There was a secret society of reformers, mainly educated Christian Arabs, in Beirut in the 1880s. A Christian Arab, Neguib Azoury, once assistant to the Pasha of Jerusalem, published a book about the "awakening of the Arab nation" in 1905 from the distant security of Paris. He is also credited with a prophetic vision of the coming clash of Zionism and Arab nationalism. The Arab Christian minority, who had willingly accepted Western education, had at first a disproportionate influence in the small but growing politically conscious groups among whom nationalism emerged as well as in the journalism which took advantage of the 1908 revolution. Some were Roman Catholic or Lebanese Maronite and so in cultural contact with the secular as well as the religious Latin world. The American University in Beirut, developed from the old missionary college, had been supplemented by a French Jesuit one. Other Palestinian, Lebanese, and Syrian Christians had been won over to the ways of evangelical Christianity. Many more, though remaining Orthodox, were restive about the religious domination of the Greeks as well as the secular rule of the Turks.

Palestine, say Arab nationalists and advocates like Father Lucas Grollenberg, was "a sub-division of this reviving Arab world". Inevitably (and matching many exaggerations on the Jewish and Christian Zionist side) they exaggerate the pace of the revival and minimise the absence of a clear Palestinian identity under the Turks, who ruled half the Holy Land in their province of Beirut and had a province of Syria which stretched to the Gulf of Akaba.

It was when Turkey went to war in 1914, and especially after it lost in 1918, that the pace of Arab revival quickened. But by then the Jewish opportunity had come in a way that might have encouraged the Zionists to quote the prophet Habakkuk's thoughts from the watchtower: "Though it tarry, wait for it; because it will surely come, it will not tarry." When it came, it came quickly.

# 7 THE RUSSIAN CONNECTION

*AN EPIC THAT REMAINS TO BE WRITTEN.....*

The Russian connection with the Holy Land deserves much more than a passing mention. It was of long standing, for there are journals of medieval Russian pilgrims who reached Jerusalem. Sir George Adam Smith's papers record an offer of help in translating them. Around the year 1600 Russian pilgrims were still claiming to see the marks of Pharaoh's chariot-wheels beside the Red Sea and were noted for their piously confused legend that Mary and the infant Jesus had stood unharmed in the middle of the burning bush seen by Moses in Sinai. Later in the seventeenth century the connection found expression in Patriarch Nikon's bid to create a replica of the Church of the Holy Sepulchre at the New Jerusalem monastery near Moscow. It was an important connection politically and diplomatically until it was abruptly broken in 1914 and never resumed in its old form, because of the events in 1917, but it was also important spiritually.

There is much about it that the West finds difficult to understand and probably still much for historians to explain. The Russians themselves were in no position between 1917 and 1990 either to explain it or understand it fully, for some of the most important strands in the connection concerned areas of human thought and experience which Communist interpretations of history and human nature despised, denied, or rejected.

When in 1913 the British writer Stephen Graham travelled with a ship-load of Russian pilgrims from Odessa he noted that they were treated with derision and even contempt by many of their countrymen in the crew, who expressed the revolutionary spirit which was only just battened down in these last years of imperial Russia. Such revolutionaries equated religion with superstition. That spirit was for 70 years after

1917 to be expressed in the Soviet Government's attitude to Russian history, as well as in the tight control which it exercised on foreign travel.

There remained a very strong Soviet diplomatic and political interest in the Middle East and some Russian imperial ambitions may have been pursued in new ways. But there were no pilgrims - or none who admitted it - among the diplomats, military advisers, consultants, and technicians who went to the Middle East. Only a few favoured church-men - those on whom the régime could depend - visited the Holy Land, though there was a Russian Orthodoxy in exile which maintained its older traditions. But despite the hard times and vexed arguments about ownership of Russian Church property, the signs of the old connection remained - whether in gilded Russian churches or the vast compound in central Jerusalem rented out to the British and then the Israelis. It was still visible occasionally in the interest which tame and even suspect Soviet churchmen - such as the late Archbishop Nikodim - sometimes showed if the World Council of Churches discussed the affairs of Jerusalem.

Who knows what form the interest will take in the future? Russia's outlook remains uncertain, but at least its past can now be acknowledged.

In the century before the First World War about a million Christian pilgrims from overseas came to Palestine. Perhaps a majority of them, and certainly the largest single national group, came from the Russian Empire. In the last years before the First World War the numbers of the Russians (including Ukrainians and other Orthodox subjects of the Czar) were between 10,000 and 15,000 annually. They travelled by the Russian steamship line from Odessa to Jaffa, crammed the Jerusalem hospices, especially at the Orthodox Easter, tramped on foot around other holy places, and bathed in the Jordan. In the fickle spring weather of 1893 a party of 760 Russian pilgrims, old women among them, set out in sunshine from Nazareth on their return journey through the hills and were caught by a belated but sharp bout of winter in mid-March. Many died by the wayside and others, carried back to the hospices of Jerusalem, never caught the return boat to Odessa.

Someone else got the 12 roubles (a bit more than £1) which they had sewn into their clothes for the fare home.

Although some Russians had for centuries mingled with the other Orthodox pilgrims, Western observers at first gave little special attention to them and lumped them all together as "Greeks". The early Victorians hardly noticed them, although the Russian Government paid for the restoration in 1840 of the Mar Saba monastery in Judea, five years after it had been plundered during a time of even greater than usual political instability. When Eliot Warburton visited it in 1847 he noted that a Russian monk lit his pipe for him and then offered a "powerful cordial in a liqueur glass" and that many of the monks spoke only Russian. Mid-Victorians, however, began to notice the Russian presence among the Orthodox pilgrims, as when Norman Macleod at the Church of the Holy Sepulchre watched "Russians from the far-off steppes of Tartary, clothed in their sheepskin dresses". Late Victorians could not fail to notice.

Many Westerners regarded the building of Russian churches and hospices as deliberate exploitation for political purposes of the claim, dating from the days of Catherine the Great and among the tangled causes of the Crimean War, that the Tsar was the protector of Orthodox subjects of the Turks. Russia was also suspected of dabbling in the internal affairs, and sometimes bitter quarrels, of Eastern Christians in the Holy Land by encouraging a movement for an Arab Orthodox Church, free of the Greek monastic domination which was still a cause of friction long after the Second World War.

At approximately the same time as Macleod's visit Canon Tristram, because he had been in Jerusalem before, noted more specifically the impact the Russians were making. He thought the new Russian compound buildings out of harmony with their suroundings and overshadowing every other architectural feature. The compound, he said, "combines in some degree the appearance and uses of cathedral close, public offices, barracks and hostelry." There were many Russian monks and priests as well as crowds of pilgrims.

Still the whole style of the group seems a sort of taking possession of the land by implication, in

strong contrast with the simple and chaste cluster on
the top of Mount Zion where the English Mission
has its centre. The Greeks view the Russian
establishment with great jealousy, not to say dislike,
and attribute it to a settled determination on the part
of the Tsar to separate the Muscovite Church
altogether from the Greek and throw off what little
dependence is still acknowledged on the Patriarchate
of Constantinople.

Sir Charles Wilson developed the same theme speaking to the
Palestine Exploration Fund in 1899. He suggested that when
the Greeks flew the Turkish flag on the tower of the Church
of the Holy Sepulchre at the previous Easter it might have
been to annoy the Russians who had sent an admiral and
detachment of sailors to the Orthodox celebration. He spoke
of the schools opened by the Russians and teaching their
language, comparing their Church policy with the one which
had helped create a national exarchate in Bulgaria, in the face
of determined Greek resistance.

But although the Russians dabbled in nationalist Church
politics, there is some evidence that the pilgrims came first and
Russian policy and Romanov patronage followed, partly to
provide for them and partly to make use of them. The Tsarist
Government had its own doubts about encouraging its people
to see the world. But on this matter at least it deferred to the
wishes of its people, even though it tried to take a political
opportunity from them.

The Russian pilgrimage was a people's occasion, largely a
peasant one: as Macleod's phrase suggests, of travellers wearing sheepskins. It seems to have developed as a lay movement
and not mainly a clerical, far less a patriarchal or episcopal one.
In the Protestant West the opinion-formers and leaders of the
Churches came - Bonar and McCheyne, Stanley, Macleod -
and reported articulately back to a literate and interested
religious public, some of whose more prosperous and leisured
members then sought estimates from Mr Cook for an inclusive trip with dragoman, camels, and visits to the Pyramids en
route. Even George Pitt wrote for Quakers back home. In

Russia the word seems to have spread by personal contact among the illiterate.

When Agnes Smith and her sister went to see the ceremony of the Holy Fire they noted that a "very bigoted Russian lady" sitting beside them also seemed to have rather sweeping views about her peasant compatriots, who formed a large part of the congregation. The Russian disclaimed belief in the "miracle" (which the Smith sisters put down to putting a light to spirits of wine) but allegedly said: "The *canaille* want to see a spectacle and would be angry if the priests did not give them it."

Westerners were baffled by the Russian people's pilgrimage. Some writers were patronising about it, keeping their distance but finding it picturesque, and a few - most notably Stephen Graham at the end of the era - were almost uncritically enthusiastic. Many were antagonised by the uncouth and even dirty appearance which the pilgrims often presented and some had more precise cause for complaint. When the Revd Wallace Brown and Mrs Brown of Alness in Ross-shire visited the Church of the Holy Sepulchre in 1896 they were objective enough to note the joy, comfort, and consolation of the Russians, but added: "Strange, but true. One of these very worshippers tried to pick the pockets of one of our party." The Browns' party had other problems with Orthodox Christians on that trip. They were shipwrecked at Zante on the return voyage and some were robbed.

One of the first detailed attempts by a Western writer to describe the Russian pilgrims is by the best-selling American travel-writer Charles Dudley Warner in 1875. Once known as "a genial exponent of the best sort of American thought", Warner was sometimes compared and contrasted with his contemporary Mark Twain. His *In the Levant* is a book of some distinction, though it covers much more than the Holy Land. His picture of the Russians is meant to be vivid and perhaps unflattering, but can be seen in a different light. He visited the new Russian compound, noting a building set apart for rich pilgrims and a larger one for peasants, who were lodged free. In the church there he saw some pictures set in frames decorated with diamonds, emeralds, and rubies presented by rich devotees, but he thought they demonstrated wealth rather than taste. However most of the pilgrims, he said, were "simple, rude, clumsy, honest boors", thick-set, padded-legged, short-bodied, and unintelligent. "These people will need to make a good many more pilgrimages, and perhaps to quit their morose land altogether, before they can fairly rank among the civilised of the earth."

He recorded that they were laden with household gear, did much mending of well-worn footwear, and wore furs and heavy woollen clothes, even when sunning themselves. Indoors the rooms were "not very savoury". But he noted the variety of Russian races, and that some had walked 2000 miles to get to Odessa. He also listed the souvenirs they were packing - not only relics, beads, and pictures, but rosemary spread out to dry, tins of Jordan water, cane-stalks from the river, and "round cakes of blessed bread stamped with the image of the Saviour". There were also the emblems of mortality especially associated with the Russian pilgrimage: skull caps for the dead and "long strips of cotton cloth stamped in black with various insignia of death to serve at home for coffin-covers."

Travellers who took the road and mixed with the local people also encountered the Russians, for example at the caravanserai on the Jericho road where the French novelist Pierre Loti in 1895 noted "huddles of Russian pilgrims, with fine bemedalled old men". The caravanserais offered accommodation of a sort for pilgrims and animals, but they provided litle else beyond fresh water, hookahs, and coffee brewed on what Loti called primitive little furnaces. The Russians were noted for their samovars and tea-drinking but on the Jericho road they were boiling up soup on twig-fires and eating their staple black bread.

Nearly 20 years later there was a striking picture, fuller than Loti's and much more sympathetic, from an evangelical English journalist, Arthur Copping, who was writing a book on the Middle East with his brother Harold as illustrator. On their way from Nablus to Bethel they encountered the Russian pilgrims in the borderland of Judea and Samaria. It cannot have been far from the scene of the disaster that overtook the column in 1893 which was probably on the same route. It was one of the processional marches across the countryside which took the Russians as far north as the Sea of Galilee and Nazareth. This group too must have been on the way back to Jerusalem. "From end to end of the Plain of Lubban the black line extended - a mile of pilgrims." It made a particular impression on the Coppings because the area where they had camped was a lonely one and their party seemed isolated in a wilderness. They had been looking across an empty, silent land before breaking camp in the morning when the jagged black line emerged through a defile.

Most of the pilgrims were old and heavy-laden with bundles wrapped round their bodies and "the one creature comfort they had brought with them". With a staff in one hand, most of the men carried a teapot in the other. The women used old umbrellas as walking-sticks. Some sought to beg food to supplement their stale Russian bread and the Coppings felt a sting of conscience, for their provisions were luxury in comparison. "We could not invite 800 guests to breakfast. And so we gently shook our heads." Later they camped close to the the pilgrim band and were disconcerted to see the Russians tackling "with a horrid complacency" the problem of getting rid of the vermin infesting their clothes. The Coppings retained happier memories of the pilgrims' open-air hymns.

About the same time another English literary pilgrim, Robert Hichens, noted the intensity of Russian pilgrim devotion. At Jacob's Well, Hichens (brother of a canon at the Jerusalem cathedral) prided himself on getting there so early in the morning that "not even a patient and pathetic Russian was before me". However when he got to the Church of the Holy Sepulchre early on the morning of Good Friday he found the Russians were there first in their hundreds, waiting all that day and night for the following day's "miracle" (of the Holy Fire) and sometimes sleeping upright. He looked by the light of the hundreds of hanging lamps at their seamed faces and hands knotted over their staves and thought of the words: "Thy rod and thy staff they comfort me."

Lady Butler was also sympathetic, when she met a group of Russian pilgrims while she was sketching at the "Shepherd's Field" near Bethlehem. One old man from Tobolsk in Siberia told her that he had been two years' on the tramp but that "he could manage his return journey in no time, only ten months or so." The two priests with the Russian party were Orthodox Arabs from Bethlehem.

The British writer Stephen Graham was much closer to the pilgrims as well as enthusiastic about them. He had been attracted to Russia by its literature (as he still proudly insisted in his *Who's Who* entry in the 1960s) and spoke the language. He was also to tramp across great areas of Russian Central Asia, writing a book of some historical value about an area where Christendom and Islam meet and where one style of Russian rule was soon to be replaced by the Soviet system which purported to replace both religions. He had learned to understand the Russian peasant way of life and popular Russian Orthodox religion, though a later book on serving during the war in the ranks of the Scots Guards indicates that he was still a Presbyterian. In 1913 he joined a pilgrimage and sailed from Odessa, travelling in a ship which had 560 such passengers in its hold. He noted that they were almost all sea-sick and served by three boltless lavatories.

He contrasted the excitement and exhilaration of the Russian pilgrimage, "the highest rite that Christianity has conceived", with the disillusionment he claimed Western visitors encountered in the Holy Land. He longed for a Russian to write a great national epic about the pilgrimage "that would make Europe ring".

Graham, a Slavophile who survived to see the end of Stalinism and the fall of Kruschev, thought he had encountered the most remarkable and significant movement in Russian life. His own account of his voyage and Holy Land travels, *With the Russian Pilgrims to Jerusalem,* is one of the most remarkable books about Palestine and pilgrimage. That it is so little known today is easily explained. Both his book and his ideas were overtaken by events. There were no pilgrim-ships in the seasons after the spring and early summer of 1914, when Graham was visiting Baku and Russian Central Asia. Soon the Russian hospices were full of other people's troops and supplies.

There was a brief revival of the old tradition after the war before Russia was fully transformed into the Soviet Union and the "new civilisation" (as the Webbs quaintly described it) curbed foreign travel and persecuted religion. The Scots medical missionary at Hebron and admirer of Graham's book, Alexander Paterson, wrote just after his own return from the war of the Russian pilgrims' welcome reappearance and "the return to the landscape of a feature that always gave it a very moving human interest". He admired their "child-like emotion that exhaled a religious fervour", and contrasted it with other pilgrims who seemed so strait-laced and sophisticated. Paterson was specially impressed by the devotion linked to the ceremony of the Holy Fire, even though "as every educated Greek acknowledges" the fire from which so many tapers were lit was produced by artifice rather than miracle. He thought less of the unseemly scenes in the church and the superstition than of the way the sacred flame was taken thousands of miles to the remotest Russian villages, kept prayerfully alive from taper to taper within lanterns.

But the times were soon out of joint. The great epic Graham longed for was never written. In a way that he could not have expected, the main Russian connection with Palestine for the rest of his long lifetime - he died in 1975 - was to be through the emigration of Russian Jews and not the visits by Russian Orthodox pilgrims.

Now the book and its ideas may come into their own again. The epic may be written after all. Perhaps it might even integrate the pilgrim devotion of Holy Russia and the Zionist flight from Tsarist Russia and Soviet Russia.

However simple and uneducated the Russian pilgrims were, even at times superstitious, they had a vision of the glory of Christ. And some of those very different enthusiasts for the Holy Land - Jews and Gentiles - who sought God's purpose in the return of people of Israel to the land of Israel saw Jesus as the fulfilment both of modern hopes and ancient promises. For example in 1882, the year on which so much emphasis is placed in Zionist interpretations of history, one of the Jews from the Russian Empire who came to Palestine to seek out possibilities of settlement was Joseph Rabinowitz of Kishinev in Bessarabia. His life and thought were to become a vital inspiration for the "Messianic Jews" found today in modern Israel and elsewhere, whose potential importance is out of proportion to their small numbers. On the Mount of Olives Rabinowitz came to see a previous visitor there as Israel's king and Messiah, and as "our brother Jesus". In his own way he affirmed what the Anglican appointment of Bishop Alexander had tried to express and what the Presbyterians Bonar and McCheyne had recognised: that acceptance of Christ was as compatible with a sense of identity and nationality for Jews as for Greeks, Scots, Russians, or Germans.

The epic of the Russian connection may encompass Messianic Jews as well as pilgrim devotion. The story is still far from its end.

# 8   WAR CHANGES EVERYTHING

*THE FLOWER OF SCOTLAND'S BATTLE FOR JERUSALEM*

Wars and rumours of wars have always been part of the history of the Holy Land, a small country in a strategic position, often on a shifting or debatable frontier. The visitor there today is told of so many wars, as well as continuing conflict, that he may lose sight of the importance of the one between 1914 and 1918 which ended 13 centuries of Muslim rule. There are few visible traces, and so much has happened since.

It is often said that war settles nothing. But it can change everything. Palestine was never the same again after the First World War. Its fate for the rest of the century, and perhaps far beyond, was determined by the battles and the politics of a war in which it was sometimes described as a "sideshow". But it was no sideshow for those who took part, among them British soldiers who - some of them, for at least some of the time - felt like pilgrims in uniform. On the other side, in support of the Turks, there were Germans and Austrians who felt the same mood. Most were Christians but some were Jews, especially in the Austrian contingent.

It was one war which might have passed Palestine by, but for the last great and fatal misjudgment of the Ottoman Empire. Despite Turkey's growing diplomatic, economic, and political affiliations with Germany, there was no direct reason for its involvement. A cool, rational Turkish calculation of the kind which had delayed the collapse of the empire might have opted for recovery from the exhaustion of the Balkan wars and could have hoped to profit from other people's disasters. But the Turks wanted Russia beaten, feared that a victorious Russia would take Constantinople, and staked everything on a German victory.

War did not come to Palestine quickly. The Turks, despite their links with Germany and a secret alliance concluded on the eve of the war, were taken aback by British involvement and waited to see how the first few months in the West turned out. They saw the Germans checked far away in France, and the stalemate which followed. They were encouraged by the arrival at Constantinople of German warships which slipped the British pursuit and irritated by the seizure of warships being built for them in Britain. Most important, on the fronts where they felt closer and more involved, they reckoned that the great German victories in East Prussia and Poland ensured Russia would fail, even against Austria-Hungary. The Turks judged that the Serbs were doomed, despite the way they had disconcerted the Austrians, and that Britain and France were too committed in the West to bring down the Ottoman Empire.

It was a high-risk policy which for three years seemed to succeed. When Turkey came into the war at the beginning of November 1914 the main British priority in the Middle East was to keep Egypt and the Suez Canal secure. That was never in doubt, though Turkish troops from Palestine made a sortie in 1915 to mount ineffective early attacks on the canal and failed with a more substantial attack in Sinai the following year. When Britain and France gathered strength in the Eastern Mediterranean they ignored Palestine and Syria in favour of what, had it been well co-ordinated and pressed home, could have been a mortal blow at Turkey. But they hesitated and delayed. The Dardanelles were not forced, and the Gallipoli expedition was checked and then evacuated. Even then troops were diverted to hold a large but ineffective bridgehead at Salonika. Although the British pushed across Sinai along the route taken by many armies, and by such travellers as Bonar and McCheyne, they again discovered the quality of Turkish troops in strong defensive positions. They also learned slowly to cope with the problems of getting supplies from Egypt, laying a railway and water-pipes behind them but also depending on long camel caravans. Two attacks at Gaza failed, and a group of British prisoners was paraded through the streets of Jerusalem. It was not until the end of October 1917 that a sufficiently powerful force with adequate artillery was committed to win the third battle of Gaza and bring the war into Palestine. But the Holy Land was still strongly defended by the Turks, encouraged first by their victory at Gallipoli and then by the collapse of Russia, which allowed them to divert their efforts from the Caucasus. They were backed by German and Austrian gunners, engineers, and specialist units, even some infantry, and were directed by a formidable German general, Erich von Falkenhayn.

Until then Palestine had known many of the tensions of war, and felt some of its cruel effects, without being fought over. It was already uneasy before the Turks committed themselves. Many of its young men had been marched away to distant wars in the Balkans or had fled to avoid conscription. The country had to bear the cost of those wars and another between the Turks and Italy. The hopes of a Turkish revival based on a liberal multi-national approach gave way to new frustration and bitterness. In Galilee the Scots and English missionaries heard rumours that Muslim fanaticism might turn against foreigners and Christians. They also noted that "there were all manner of Germans in Tiberias and that there was no mistaking their attitude. It was that of men in possession."

When the wider war came those who felt the effects first, but probably suffered least, were the British who worked in Palestine. Before the end of August 1914 the London Church Missions to Jews told their British staff to leave. On September 7 the British consul-general sent a messenger to Dr David Torrance at the Scots hospital in Tiberias urging him to do the same. He did, taking all the British staff, and with some difficulty managed to reach Port Said by ship from Haifa. A Swiss nursing sister was left in charge. In Jerusalem Canon Hichens of the cathedral and the headmaster of St George's School lingered too long and needed the intervention of the American consul to help them out. In the American colony the Vesters took charge of the crosses and chalices of St George's and the title deeds of French Roman Catholic properties. But they fell out with the German community at the Lutheran Sunday afternoon open-house coffee-party, which already had army officers among the guests. Bertha

Vester's husband Frederick, though of American outlook and pro-British sentiments, was still a German national.

But long before the fighting moved into Palestine itself in 1917, it had become a cruel war for those Turkish subjects, Jewish and Arab, who were thought to sympathise with the British.

The desert revolt of the Arabs, encouraged and sustained by the British and associated especially with T.E. Lawrence, spread from what is now Saudi Arabia into Jordan and Syria. It reached the fringe of Palestine when Lawrence's force occupied Akaba, now in Jordan near the modern Israeli Eilat, in May 1917. Although the revolt tied down Turkish troops it had little direct political impact on Palestine. At the end of the war those Arab-Turkish officers who sympathised with nationalism were still generally fighting for the Ottoman Empire, and not surprisingly the new Arab political ferment was centred on the great cities of Baghdad and Damascus, not Jerusalem. But many Arabs suffered from the rigour of Turkish martial law. In Jerusalem several accused of pro-Allied activities, including a Mufti of Gaza and his son, were hanged outside the Jaffa Gate. The executioners posed proudly for a ghastly photograph reproduced from the Jerusalem municipality archives in Martin Gilbert's historical photo-atlas. There were 11 such executions in 1915 and 21 more in January 1916, allegedly as a result of incriminating documents seized from the French consulate. Suffering of a different kind came to Arabs as well as Jews from the diseases, including an outbreak of cholera, which flourished amid food shortages.

But the war brought even more havoc to the Jewish minority in Palestine. In Jerusalem many who stayed were sick and close to starvation. But many were not allowed to stay. There were Turkish deportations of Jews from Jaffa and the coastal strip and an emigration of refugees to Egypt. "We waited for the English", wrote a Jew who stayed, Joseph Baratz of the Degania *kibbutz* near the Jordan's exit from the Sea of Galilee. He had been the first bridegroom married there; the second was the father of the Israeli general Moshe Dayan. One of their colleagues was Joseph Trumpeldor, once a Russian soldier but who now became a British captain. He was the animating spirit of the Zion Mule Corps - a Jewish unit, recruited from Egyptian and refugee Palestinian Jews, which served at Gallipoli. But the Jews who remained behind were closely watched and harried by the Turks, though their hardships were eased by presents from Jewish soldiers in the German and Austrian units supporting the Turks. Baratz himself was arrested and beaten and he recorded that his friends Rosa Aaronson and her brother, involved with British intelligence, were tortured to death without betraying their contacts.

The British were a long time coming, even to Jerusalem. The army under General Allenby, who had been transferred from France earlier in the year, finally won the third battle of Gaza on November 7, 1917 and in less than 10 days had moved into what George Adam Smith called the "great warpath" of the Plain of Sharon and had taken Jaffa. But as every reader of the Bible knows, the pilgrim goes *up* to Jerusalem, a city set on hills and dominated by others. That meant that Allenby's army had to fight its way into the hills, roughly along the traditional pilgrim route, and then secure the dominating heights, especially Nebi Samwil, where half a century before Norman Macleod had been so amazed and elated by the view. The advance was quick enough to secure the vital access to the hills, but could not hope to manoeuvre the Turks out of Jerusalem. A battle was inevitable.

Allenby led what Winston Churchill later called "brilliant and frugal operations". From the historian's viewpoint that verdict has much force. Neither the numbers of men involved nor the proportion who became casualties in a single battle compared with what happened on the Western Front. But the perspective of the troops who fought on the ridges, slopes, and ravines of Judea was rather different. "Frugal" meant that depleted battalions went into attack after attack. The same units went into battle more often. They had shorter rests and fewer replacements (for the sick as well as the dead and wounded) as well as fewer reliefs and reserves. Battalions did not lose most of their strength in one attack, as happened in France, but they were worn down as the fighting went on. The most comparable fighting of the Second World War was probably the lot of an infantry battalion fighting its way up Italy.

There were Australians and some New Zealanders in
Allenby's large cavalry force, partly on the desert flank, and
seven British infantry divisions, among them Welsh and East
Anglians. But the Territorial division which was to have the
key role in the battle for Jerusalem was the Scottish Lowland
52nd. Thanks to regimental tradition some of the "Lowlanders"
were Highland Light Infantry and Argyll and Sutherland
Highlanders who had kilts. They were to be glad of them on
cold November nights of 1917 when neighbouring battalions
of Royal Scots, King's Own Scottish Borderers, Cameronians,
and Royal Scots Fusiliers shivered in drill jackets and shorts.

The 52nd had been to Gallipoli and knew about the Turks
and about casualties. But when it fought at Gaza and in Judea
it retained its character in a way that no division in France
could have done in the autumn of 1917. Being a Territorial
Division, the 52nd had a core of pre-war volunteers and even
the drafts with replacements had not jumbled up the regi-
ments as happened in France. This was still - to use a much
later phrase - the flower of Scotland, or at least of Lowland
Scotland. It was far above the army's average in education,
discipline, and morale and drew many of its officers and men
from the kind of young Scots who were still raised on the Bible
and may have had Andrew Bonar's *Palestine for the Young* as
a Sunday school prize. When one of its officers told a relief
from an Indian division that the best guide to the countryside
was the Bible - unconsciously echoing Bonar's conversation in
1839 with Sir Moses Montefiore - he probably meant it.

Many of the officers came from Scotland's urban middle
class. Others were countrymen and even county types, for the
4th R.S.F. organised a mounted fox-hunt somewhere in
today's suburbs of Tel Aviv. But the spirit of the division
spread all round the ranks and its survivors remembered the
comradeship as well as the ordeals. It could still be encountered long afterwards. Once, for example, I published some
favourable comments on the Israeli withdrawal from Sinai
and was startled by the vigour of an aged Presbyterian veteran
who wrote at great length about the folly of giving up the
strategic area he had marched across in 1917. But that spirit is
also inscribed in the well-worn divisional history that has
provided some of the references for this chapter: "T.B

Somerville, 11 Platoon, 3 Coy., 1/7 Batt., Royal Scots, 156
Brigade, 52 Lowland Div. 1917-18."

There are not many units in which the divisional history
- once common in Scots second-hand bookshops, now scarcer
- sells down to the level of the ordinary soldier whose war
memories are not of strategy and tactics but of 11 Platoon.

This was not an ironsided division of Puritans, and perhaps some of those who survived and remembered added
embellishments. Did men who had to take time from their
own troubles to shoot camels that fell into ravines also take
time to talk about the Crusaders? Perhaps not. Yet the army
command, sensitive to Muslim and Jewish sensitivities, had to
order, apparently in vain, that the word was not to be used.
Did the rest of the 5th K.O.S.B. agree with the writer of the
battalion's war diary who wrote that "their hearts burned
within them as they heard the chimes of the clock on the
tower of the modern Latin Franciscan monastery" at the
supposed Emmaus? Possibly not, but there is a cry from the
heart when he notes that some of the men had not heard
church-bells since they left Scotland. Did men whose boots
were worn out and bound up with string and bits of puttees
agree with the officer who recorded that "the peaks that had
seen the hundred holy battles around Jerusalem stood over us
in judgment"? Perhaps not always. A regimental chaplain
noted that the soldier fighting across parched plains and bare
hills didn't think this a land of milk and honey "and had no
hesitation in stating his opinion". The divisional historian
who recorded that the men liked singing hymns might have
added "and much else besides". An English officer, Clement
Hankey, who marched from Egypt via El Arish and Gaza
recorded that the army found the most appropriate song was:
> There's a long, long trail goes winding
> To the land of my dreams.

Yet there is a ring of authenticity about the 52nd Division's
account of services in the dark at which only very familiar
metrical psalms and paraphrases could be sung. A light to see
the words on a hymn-sheet could have brought down enemy
fire. These were men who had enough verses from memory to

lift up their voices, as well as their eyes, to the hills around
Jerusalem.

There was a fierce battle for Nebi Samwil, even after its
capture, for the Turks counter-attacked, knowing that it
would settle the fate of Jerusalem. The Scots won, but it was
two sergeants from a London battalion who encountered the
mayor carrying the white flag of truce, on December 9.
Grumbling about others getting the glory, the 52nd moved
back to the coast, some of them billeted at what their historian
mistakenly thought was the German-Jewish colony of Sarona
near Jaffa. It was German, but Protestant, and its peaceful
people became more victims of war. The men had gone north
with the Turks and the women were interned. Nearby at
Rishon-le-Zion an English Yeomanry officer, Robert Wilson,
whose squadron had been detached from the desert flank for
escort duty at corps headquarters, identified the nature of the
settlement there correctly enough. He found all the people
around were Jews, bought 40 oranges for a shilling, but
complained that "they nearly faint if you try to buy anything
from them on their sabbath". Discipline and good relations
were served, however, by leaving the money on the table.

Two days after Jerusalem's surrender came one of the
supreme symbolic moments in its secular history. In one of
the great gestures of military diplomacy and public relations,
General Allenby entered Jerusalem on foot through the Jaffa
Gate. There was a deliberate contrast with the Kaiser's mounted pomp and circumstance of nearly 20 years before. French
and Italian representatives had been summoned in the interests of Allied solidarity and there were places of honour for the
dignitaries of Jerusalem's various religions and communities.

Among the military spectators was T.E. Lawrence, who
had hitherto thought Jerusalem a squalid town, robbed of its
character by pilgrims and Zionists. It was not one of the cities
providing his "seven pillars of wisdom". He thought these
"united forces of the past and future" had denied the city any
present identity, and found its people remote from ideals of
Arab nationality and as characterless as hotel servants. But
even Lawrence felt the sense of occasion, and decided that he
must not miss "the supreme moment of the war". For such a
moment he eschewed his Arab costume and borrowed a

major's uniform with brass hat and red tabs, the last lent by Lord Dalmeny, the future Earl of Rosebery. As he drove back to camp Lawrence felt shamefaced with triumph and, then or later, thought up fine phrases for the *Seven Pillars of Wisdom* about the sunshine of a great thankfulness and a saluting mountainside.

The ceremonies completed, Jerusalem settled down under its latest conquerors. Indian Muslim troops were placed as a diplomatic cordon round the Haram. The Army Service Corps set up an ice factory near the Zion Gate, where the Turks had once insulted the Jews with the stink of their slaughter-house. At the Kaiserin Augusta Victoria German hospice, recently the enemy headquarters, services in the chapel were resumed, but in English and with a London Scottish private acting as organist. Troops who had leisure did some sight-seeing at holy places, though a Royal Artillery major warned Siegfried Sassoon (briefly in Palestine after his convalescence): "Don't go to the Garden of Gethsemane. It's the duddest show I've ever seen." But others who had the chance even risked walking tours: Clement Hankey and another officer disregarded cautionary voices and headed for the "exceptionally fanatical" area around Hebron. On the way they found a Salesian mission-school at Beit Gemal where Italian monks gave them wine and fruit. At Hebron they met nothing worse than some spitting, apparently directed at a Jew "with corkscrew curls" who had constituted himself their guide. A boy from Bethlehem asked them when the British would reach Acre, for his parents were there.

Beyond Jerusalem and on the coast the campaign had continued, but with only one last Palestinian battle for the Scots Territorials. They forced the river they called the Auja but which today's Tel Aviv guides call by the Hebrew name of Yarkon. The brigades erected monuments to mark their crossings, one of them beside the future site of a Tel Aviv power-station. But they were then recalled to fight in France, where many a survivor of the Gaza and Judean battles found death or wounds, leaving their Scots gunners behind to join an Indian division and end their war far to the north of Beirut.

By then Allenby had fought a fresh campaign, almost forgotten now but which in its day and the aftermath of the

Western Front stalemate excited such military pundits as Basil
Liddell Hart, who thought it a masterpiece of movement and
initiative. In the first stage of this last offensive the Scots
painter James McBey, sent from the Western Front to be a
"war artist", sketched a kilted Highland battalion starting an
attack by moonlight at Jelil, close to the present highway from
Tel Aviv to Haifa. But the Turkish army was finally routed
south-west of Nazareth at Megiddo - otherwise Armageddon
and scene of so many battles that its name had become a
symbol of war itself. The Arabs who had fought with Lawrence, and many who had more recently abandoned the
Turks, hoped for the fruits of victory in Damascus.

But Jews too hoped for the fruits of victory. At Degania
Joseph Baratz welcomed the Australian cavalry, who got on
well with the settlers, and experienced "a heady joy", thinking
a new Jewish State was already in existence. "A new spirit was
blowing through the land and we waited eagerly for the
immigrant ships." David Torrance of Tiberias was feeling the
cold in Glasgow and fretting to get back to his Galilee hospital.

The war had changed everything, but settled nothing.
Commitments and conflicting expectations from the war
years were to bring Palestine an uneasy peace and, in no very
distant future, different wars. To understand what later travellers and pilgrims were to encounter in Palestine, it is necessary to look at what the politicians were doing while the
soldiers were bringing their supplies across Sinai, forcing the
lines at Gaza, and settling the fate of Jerusalem on Nebi
Samwil.

The Balfour Declaration of support for a Jewish "national
home" had been issued on November 2, 1917, one of the
crucial days of the Third Battle of Gaza.

# 9 A DECLARATION OF AMBIGUITY

*HIS MAJESTY'S GOVERNMENT VIEW WITH FAVOUR THE
ESTABLISHMENT IN PALESTINE OF A NATIONAL HOME FOR
THE JEWISH PEOPLE, AND WILL USE THEIR BEST
ENDEAVOURS TO FACILITATE THE ACHIEVEMENT OF THIS
OBJECT, IT BEING CLEARLY UNDERSTOOD THAT NOTHING
SHALL BE DONE WHICH MAY PREJUDICE THE CIVIL AND
RELIGIOUS RIGHTS OF THE EXISTING NON-JEWISH
COMMUNITIES IN PALESTINE, OR THE RIGHTS AND
POLITICAL STATUS ENJOYED BY JEWS IN ANY OTHER
COUNTRY.*

That declaration of intent which the British Foreign Secretary, Arthur Balfour, made in a letter to Lord Rothschild on November 2, 1917 was brief, significant, and ambiguous. It was described as a "declaration of sympathy with Jewish Zionist aspirations" that had been approved by the British Cabinet. It was meant to be passed on to the Zionist Federation. From it flowed the events that led to the creation of the State of Israel and the unresolved conflict of Jews and Arabs in Palestine.

Its background may now seem relatively ancient history as well as utterly remote from the interests and inclinations of those who travel as pilgrims or tourists to the Holy Land. But it determined the nature of the State they find there and led to the conflicts of which even the most unworldly pilgrim soon becomes aware. The visitor who wants to know something about the land today needs to know something of the Balfour Declaration.

At the time the letter was sent there was uncertainty about when and how the declaration of sympathy could be given practical expression, as well as about the form a national home would take and its relation to the "existing non-Jewish communities of Palestine".

The most immediate uncertainties, however, did not arise from the ambiguity of the declaration and the reaction of Muslims and Christians in Palestine. They were uncertainties about the result of the war and the nature of the peace to follow.

The declaration was a unilateral British act, although it had American sympathy. It did not at first commit the Allies as a whole, and there were French interests and ambitions that would certainly figure in a peace settlement. But in the autumn of 1917 the British army was bogged down in Flanders and the French army was conserving what remained of its strength. The Russians had stumbled out of the war and Lenin's Bolsheviks were seizing power. The Germans could move troops from the East and mount one last great offensive before the Americans brought their power to bear. There was no certainty that the Allies would be able to dictate terms, and military stalemate might raise the possibility of a compromise peace.

Palestine, for the moment, was not only a Turkish territory in law but still held by the Turkish army. But behind the Balfour Declaration lay the conviction which shaped the complex and at times contradictory British policies in the Middle East during the First World War. The Times had echoed official thinking when it reacted to the Turkish intervention on the German side: "Turkey", it said, "has pronounced its own death sentence."

For almost a century British policy had striven officiously to keep the dying Ottoman Empire alive. It was now free to change direction, even forced to do so. But it remained unsure where to go. The most immediate reversal of traditional policy was acceptance that Tsarist Russia might dominate and even acquire Constantinople. The next was to reach a concordat with the French, who had long claimed cultural and political influence in Syria and Lebanon. By 1916 an accord (the Sykes-Picot agreement) had been reached by which the area of modern Irak and Syria would be divided into British and French spheres of influence and Jerusalem, with a part of

Palestine, would be earmarked for some kind of international administration. This last point reflected Russian concerns.

But the British had also begun to assist an Arab revolt, partly influenced (according to Sir Edward Grey, the then Foreign Secretary) by a desire to create a new Arabian-based "independent Muslim political unit" centred on the Muslim holy places of Mecca and Medina. That was influenced by two factors which post-imperial Britain overlooks. The first was concern about the mood of Muslims in the British Empire, especially in India. The second was apprehension about the influence on Muslims everywhere of the Caliphate, the spiritual authority claimed by the Sultan in Constantinople. These factors helped the British Government to encourage the Grand Sherif Hussein of Mecca in his revolt, and to imply that he would win Syria and Irak, though there was an ill-expressed qualification in the correspondence with Sir Henry MacMahon, British High Commissioner in Egypt, about areas west of Damascus. This clearly included Lebanon. It was not so clear that it included Palestine, and the MacMahon correspondence has been the occasion for much acrimony as well as historical argument. The pledges which the Arabs thought they had were at odds both with the bilateral British-French understanding and the later commitment to the Jewish national home, as the Zionists understood it.

By 1917, however, another factor which Britain had never forgotten had become more important: Zionism. Events had also removed the Russian influence on the future of Jerusalem. But the policy which produced the Balfour Declaration can only be understood if we again escape from the perspectives of our own time. The evangelical Protestant tradition in British life, and the Victorian enthusiasm for Jewish missions of men like Shaftesbury and Bonar had created a receptivity to Zionism. The Zionist leader and first Israeli President, Chaim Weizmann, oversimplified and overstated matters when he wrote that "men like Balfour, Churchill, Lloyd George were deeply religious and believed in the Bible.... to them the return of the Jews to Palestine was a reality." But he was not wholly mistaken, even if he did not know that the Conservative leader of the day, Andrew Bonar Law, had been called after a missionary to the Jews.

However what is hardest to grasp now is not that Zionism
was already a powerful influence, but that it was not necessarily one aligned on the Allied side. For in 1914 the great enemy
of the Zionists was not Germany but Russia. Not long before
Herzl had tried to enlist the Kaiser, rather than the British, as
his preferred sponsor for a Jewish Palestine. The mass support
for Zionism came from Russian Jews who felt aliens in their
empire, and who were anti-imperial nationalists as well as (for
the most part) socialists of some sort. German and Austro-
Hungarian Jews were far more integrated. Except for a minority of revolutionary inclinations, they were usually as ready to
identify with their countries' war aims as their equivalents in
Britain, the "establishment" Jews of political and professional
standing like Rufus Isaacs and Edwin Montagu who were so
opposed to Zionism.

In France the rich and influential Jewish community had
not drawn Herzl's conclusions from the Dreyfus case. It
wanted to stay French. In the United States (neutral to 1917)
much of the Jewish community had come from the Russian
Empire with bitter and still quite recent memories. Most of it
might shed its socialism but not its anti-Russian Zionism.

Four considerations ensured that when the decisive moment came Zionism was aligned with the Allies. The first was
that British sympathy which Weizmann tended to overstate.
The second was the liberation of Britain, but not Germany,
from any need to worry about Turkish sovereignty in Palestine. The third was that Russia was fading out of the war just
as the United States was joining in. There was no longer a need
to defer to Russian views in planning the future of Jerusalem.
The fourth, by no means the least, was that Chaim Weizmann
had become passionately pro-British during his surprisingly
happy years at Manchester, at that time a city of world
significance, thanks to its industries, its politicians, and The
Manchester Guardian. Weizmann was devoting his talents as
a chemist to the British war effort and he was finding that his
calculations of Zionist political advantage happily coincided
with his personal pro-British preferences.

Weizmann was a brilliant lobbyist who had already made
some impact before the war on Balfour, then a Manchester
Member of Parliament. Now he had a wide range of influence,

including links to Lloyd George and Winston Churchill. Weizmann was ready to gamble on a British victory in the way the Turks had gambled on a German one, and his judgment was right. But even without him the possibility of a Jewish Palestine would have been raised in Britain as soon as the Turks became enemies. The first tentative move within the British Government for a Jewish-dominated Palestine came from Herbert Samuel, another of Asquith's Ministers. "The infant Samuel", as his friend Churchill dubbed him, was a Jew whom Weizmann had mistakenly assumed to take the Isaacs-Montagu line. His proposal to the Prime Minister was for a British annexation to encourage large-scale Jewish settlement, and for the time being it came to nothing. Asquith was indifferent to Zionism, though Samuel was determined enough to try again after both he and Asquith were out of office, and he got a warmer response from the arch-imperialist Viscount Milner in the War Cabinet. Milner became one of the most pro-Zionist of British politicians and his influential "Round Table" group speculated on the idea of a British Protectorate "able to grow into a British Dominion".

By 1917 Weizmann was also discussing the idea of a British Protectorate and the nature of a "national home", finding a responsive ear in Lord Robert Cecil, deputy to Balfour at the Foreign Office. The Zionist leader had politely declined French overtures for a Protectorate under their auspices and found that the British and the French were both having second thoughts about the part of their earlier agreement - leaked to him by C.P. Scott of The Manchester Guardian - which would have separated an internationalised or Anglo-French Jerusalem from a Galilee attached to Syria. He used the strategic argument about the added security offered to the Suez canal, secured valuable American Jewish support from the notable and influential Judge Brandeis, and discovered that the final obstacle to be overcome was that of the Jewish sceptics in high places.

Such - in brief summary - is the background to the Balfour Declaration, which under the pressures of war was published before the British Government had either secured the power to enforce it or worked out how it was to be implemented, especially in relation to the potential conflict between the

builders of the national home and the "existing non-Jewish
commuities" in Palestine.

Ever since it was issued the declaration has been surrounded by passionate controversy. Arabs and their sympathisers
portray it as the great blunder or betrayal. Israelis interpret it
in the light of what it led to - perhaps logically and inevitably
- even more than of what it actually said. Succeeding generations in Britain may wonder how their Government came to
advocate the apparently irreconcilable positions of securing
the rights of the existing Palestinian majority and sponsoring
a dramatic change in the character of the country. These are
questions which force themselves on the modern pilgrim or
traveller in Palestine and the Land of Israel - and which began
to perplex their predecessors as soon as Allenby had captured
Jerusalem. The answers usually offered reflect the partisan-
ship of the pilgrim, and the advice he receives on the spot
almost invariably reflects the politics and nationality of the
adviser. This is not the place to argue such a case, but there are
six points which are so often ignored in the argument that they
are worth making. They are overlooked because those who
note how much the Holy Land has changed, for good or ill or
a mixture of both, sometimes fix their eyes so firmly on
Palestine or Israel that they forget the extent to which the
wider world changed too, and the speed of the changes.

The first and least important is that in 1917 Palestine was
not an existing unit of government. It was much spoken of but
had to be defined - which is why Lloyd George is said to have
depended on the maps of George Adam Smith.

The second, of no moral weight but some historical force,
is that a long succession of conquerors had imposed their will
on Palestine. The concern for the rights of the existing
communities expressed by Balfour was a distinct advance on
the way the right of conquest had been exercised in the past.

Thirdly, and more important, there was no Palestinian
nation. The Balfour Declaration was right in speaking of
communities. The largest of these communities, the Muslim
one, had generally thought itself as part of an Islamic political
and spiritual empire under Turkish rule. Those Muslims and
Christians influenced by nationalism thought of themselves as
Arabs, not Palestinians, and - as subsequent Arab history was

to show - were a long way from giving practical expression to the dream of a great united Arab nation. Palestinian nationalism, as distinct from Arab feeling, only emerged later as a reaction against the Zionism that created the State of Israel.

Fourthly, there was a good deal of ignorance on both sides of the Atlantic, and perhaps among some of the Zionists themselves, about the complexities of the Holy Land and the practical as well as the longterm political difficulties in face of establishing the Jewish national home. The British Government was reasonably well informed, not least because one of its advisers was George Adam Smith, who kept in his papers a note that Allenby had been given a set of Smith's books and maps by Lloyd George and responded: "The fellow who wrote these should be in the army and not in the Church."

The Government had also turned to Smith as a very high-class propaganda consultant. The Smith papers include a revealing correspondence with Charles Masterman, an old political associate of Lloyd George now in charge of British propaganda, who was eager in October 1918 for "a very vigorous extension of publicity" and promised that if Smith would write something it would be widely circulated throughout America and in the East. It gives the impression that the Government, having rushed into a policy, was now anxious to find some arguments to support it.

Smith replied by drawing attention to a pamphlet which he had written the previous year and which in retrospect reads like a cautionary commentary on the Balfour Declaration and the mood which produced it. He was pro-Jewish and a great admirer of the Jewish development he had seen in Palestine since his first visit but (so his son Lord Balerno told me long afterwards) was concerned about the impact of a sudden surge of Jewish immigration. "I remember him speaking to me about it. He was worried about the effect on the *fellahin* - he used the Arabic word."

The pamphlet echoed passages in the *Historical Geography* by warning that Palestine was not the national home of the Jewish people only and of no other people; and that it was "useless to compare the claims of the Jews on Palestine with the rights of the Belgians to Belgium." What Smith expected was increased Jewish immigration and "a certain degree of autonomy" in a Jewish area of West Palestine, by which he meant the area west of the Jordan as distinct from Moab: that is, in the Holy Land.

This cautious view has to be set in the context of perhaps the most important of these points about the Balfour Declaration. At the end of the First World War almost everyone exaggerated the strength and the durability of British imperial power. In 1919 the British Empire may already have begun its decline in power, but it reached its greatest territorial extent. The assumptions about its durability affected not only calculation of the time-scale of change in Palestine itself, but of future spheres of influences in the Middle East and the strategic role of Palestine in imperial British communications to India and the Far East. There was an undercurrent of British interest in the strategic importance of Palestine from well before the First World War until the last days of the Mandate, though its greatest influence in Whitehall seems to have been exerted in 1945 rather than 1918.

Although after the First World War British rule in Palestine was to be called a Mandate and not a Protectorate, it was not unreasonable to regard it as part of the Empire, even at times to discuss its future in terms of "Dominion status". The apparent solidity of British rule made it possible to avoid the awkward question of whether a Jewish national home meant a Jewish State or whether such an autonomous "home" could flourish in an Arab-dominated State. The British politicians who later claimed that they envisaged a national home but not an independent Jewish State, perhaps varying their emphasis according to the time and the audience, were neither deliberately dishonest nor exceptionally stupid. Indeed Balfour, Churchill, Milner, Samuel, and Lloyd George were unusually able men. But the need to resolve the ambiguity of the Balfour Declaration seemed at the time of the peace settlement to be capable of deferment far beyond the normal time-scale for political decisions. The British Empire seemed likely to endure a long time. However the imperial factor also meant that when Britain came to implement the Balfour Declaration it faced not only the problems within Palestine but those which arose from relations with the rest of the Arab world and even the Muslims of India.

There was one final factor, hardly noticed in relation to Palestine at the time, which made it much more difficult to implement the Balfour Declaration than seemed likely at the time it was incorporated into the 1919 peace settlement. Despite a brief flurry of American interest, and even the despatch of an American commission of inquiry, it was correctly assumed that the United States was neither a rival bidder for the Mandate nor anxious to join a condominium. But it *was* assumed that it would share in the overall implementation of the peace settlement, and reflect the influence of American Protestantism's long-standing constructive interest in the Middle East and American Jewry's support for Zionist aspirations.

Instead America turned against the great Presbyterian President Woodrow Wilson, whose illness and obstinacy made matters worse. The United States declined to join the League of Nations to which Britain, as mandatory Power for Palestine, was theoretically responsible, and took little strategic or diplomatic interest in the Middle East. American influence only became significant when the Palestine question became one of who would win the battle when the Mandate ended, and when sympathy with Zionism and Jewish refugees mattered more than State Department calculations about Saudi Arabian oil prospects.

In 1919 these troubles were a long way off. The most urgent problems of the victors in the Middle East did not directly affect Palestine, once it was clear that the British would have the Mandate under the League of Nations for the administration of Palestine and the area to the east of it - beyond the Jordan and stretching across the desert to meet Irak, as Mesopotamia was now to be known. Damascus, not Jerusalem, was the most immediate goal of Arab nationalism and cause of conflict. The most powerful Arab sense of betrayal came not from events in Palestine - ominous though the first signs of local Arab protest and unrest were - but from the French insistence on their Mandate in Syria and Lebanon, which led to the humiliating expulsion of Lawrence's ally Feisal (Hussein's son) from his newly-acquired Syrian throne. That, and neither the Balfour Declaration nor the plans for the Palestine Mandate, was what seems to have encouraged T.E.

Lawrence in his strange compulsion to drop out of public life and into a curious role as a ranker in the Army and the Royal Air Force who wanted to become a great writer rather than a great hero. Lawrence, despite his dislike of the new Jerusalem, was no arch-enemy of Zionism.

The Jews too did not get all they wanted. The relatively moderate and pragmatic Weizmann tried to have Palestine defined so as to include parts of what became Lebanon and Transjordan. Some Zionist enthusiasts wanted a vaster area. The British plan was to confine the implications of the Balfour Declaration to the area generally thought of as the Holy Land. In this area the World Zionist Organisation, which had an executive body in Palestine, was recognised as the Jewish agency for "all matters pertaining to the upbuilding of the Jewish national home". Thus in a sense Palestine had an embryo or shadow Jewish administration of sorts from the earliest days of the Mandate, although the country was technically under military government until July 1920 and the Mandate was not formally transferred to the League of Nations until September 1923. It incorporated the terms and the ambiguities of the Balfour Declaration.

The real decisions had been taken much earlier in the Allied Supreme Council, and by the vigour with which the French turned King Feisal out of Damascus in 1920, set up their adminstration in Syria, and established "Grand Lebanon". Some of the decisions, however, had to be revised under the impact of events - notably in settling matters in the area east of the Jordan which was under British control but assumed at first to be part of Feisal's Syria. When Feisal was frustrated the British had to improvise - at one stage even setting up a splendidly styled but insubstantial "National Government of Moab" - and worked with some success to create a friendly Arab State in what had always been a turbulent area. The result was the emergence of Transjordan - eventually the Kingdom of Jordan.

The delays between the decisions about boundaries and the League formalities had not, however, been mainly the result of the Arab question, far less the Jewish one, but of the unexpected difficulty in imposing a peace treaty on Turkey. A new nationalism was emerging there which was ultimately, under Kemal Atatürk, to defeat Greek plans to expand into Asia Minor and lead to a wave of "ethnic cleansing".

Meanwhile between the Jordan and the sea the ambiguities of the Balfour Declaration were only too apparent. The friction which had begun to develop between the Zionists and the military administration continued under the Mandate Government. There were not enough Jewish immigrants to allow the national home to make the spectacular progress the Zionists had hoped for, but there were more than enough to enrage the Arabs and stimulate their resistance. There were also enough to provide the nucleus for the future State of Israel.

With benefit of hindsight it is easy to see that the "national home" was bound to become a Jewish State if it was to survive, and that the Arabs would never peacefully have accepted such a development. But in 1917 it was not unreasonable to think in different terms, either of a Protectorate within the British Empire or of one secured by the transformation of the wartime alliance into the basis for a League of Nations. It can be argued even more powerfully that the British Government issued the declaration, and the allies accepted it, with grossly inadequate consideration of the practical difficulties that were bound to lie ahead. But perhaps if the declaration had not been made hastily and almost recklessly it would never have been made at all.

# PART THREE: THE LAND OF ISRAEL

## 10   BRITAIN'S THANKLESS MANDATE

### *FROM ALLENBY TO HITLER*

"I justify this book by saying that what it shows will not be seen again", wrote the Oxford poet Edward Thompson in the 1920s. He had been a chaplain with the 7th Indian Division and had carried a two-volume edition of Smith's *Historical Geography* through the campaign. When he returned to Palestine and Syria to write his elegiac *Crusader's Coast*, his thoughts returned to "the Land as it was when the war ended, before progress laid its hands on it." He wanted a Palestine Preservation Trust, in which "even the most fervid Zionist might see a friend and not a foe".

Under the British Mandate progress and Zionism were changing Palestine out of all recognition. The standard Roman Catholic guide, the work of the French Father Barnabas Meistermann, told readers that long practical instructions about travel were no longer necessary as "under the British Palestine will become more and more Europeanised". The population was increasing, by natural increase as well as Jewish immigration. There seems also to have been some Arab immigration. For a time the Arab minority in Jerusalem increased as a proportion of the city's population, perhaps because Tel Aviv was expanding as a new Jewish commercial capital, rich in vigour and character but scarcely an aesthetic triumph. Jerusalem developed comparatively slowly, a trend which had one permanent benefit. It proved possible to sustain the conservationist and environmental approach of the first British governor, Sir Ronald Storrs, who ensured that Jerusalem was to remain a city of stone. Storrs ran into much criticism, not least from Zionists, but he has an honoured place in the city's history. He also gave one memorable epigram to the English literature of the Holy Land: "There is no promotion after Jerusalem."

But throughout Palestine, and especially in the areas of Jewish settlement, the economy was developing. Communications improved. The Hebrew University was opened on Mount Scopus in 1925 by Arthur (now Lord) Balfour and for the first time in the modern era the Holy Land became a centre of intellectual and scientific life. A corrupt and inefficient imperial power had been replaced by one which, whatever its faults, was honest, dedicated, competent, and doing its best to be fair.

The Mandate lasted for nearly 30 years. It is probably still too soon to see it in historical perspective. It was conceived in ambiguity, developed in indecision, and expired in conflict and almost in despair. From 1933 its problems were overshadowed by the approach of war as well as by a threat to European Jewry which could scarcely have been conceived of in 1919. But the Mandate did allow the creation of what had been so ill-defined, the Jewish national home. "What did it mean?", asked Bernard Fergusson, one of the noblest servants of Mandate Palestine. "Protection? An enclave? Sovereignty?" That was never quite clear. The eventual definition had to be determined by force.

Yet it was the Mandate years which laid foundations on which the State of Israel could be built - and which allowed a new, troubled, but tenacious Hashemite Kingdom to emerge beyond the Jordan.

Some of the changes which most immediately affected travellers were the direct result of the war. When Cook's produced a new edition of their handbook, revised by Sir Harry Luke who had been assistant governor of Jerusalem, it noted that the new railway link with Egypt meant it was no longer necessary to "undergo the ordeal of landing at Jaffa".

Every weekday through trains with sleeping and dining cars left Kantara East on the Suez Canal for Jerusalem and Haifa, the Jerusalem trains branching off at Lydda Junction. Trains for Egypt left Jerusalem at 8.15 a.m. There was even a branch line to Nablus and a link from Haifa through the plain of Esdraelon and Galilee to join up with the Hedjaz railway to Damascus, now restored from the condition to which T.E. Lawrence had reduced it. Cook's still offered Victorias drawn by two or three horses abreast, and donkeys for short excursions around Jerusalem. But the dragoman was now in charge of tours by car, or by "motors" of various sizes. A bit down-market from Cook's the motor bus was also taking advantage of the roads improved during the war or in the Mandate's early years. Soon the buses were to threaten the slow trains on the restricted railway network. They were also to reflect the division of the country's communities, as they do to this day. There were to be Arab buses and the Jewish buses which were to become vital links of the developing national home and vulnerable targets as the troubles turned to war.

A sign of the times was that three of "the principal hotels in the country" were now in Tel Aviv, and only half of the main hotels in Jerusalem were in the Old City. Another was that Hebrew as well as Arabic had become an official language along with English. All three languages appeared on the dull definitive issue of stamps (four designs showing Rachel's Tomb, the Dome of the Rock, the Jerusalem citadel and the Sea of Galilee) which replaced the military government issues and served for more than 20 years till the end of the Mandate, never varied by any commemorative issues. The mail, like other communication, depended on Egypt, the main despatches to Britain catching a weekly P.& O. mail steamer at Port Said. The Mandate was well established before air mail became important, again mainly via Egypt, though from the early 1920s there was an air mail link with Irak - only fortnightly at first. The Mandate also made do for a time with Egyptian money, before it had a Palestinian pound, reckoning in piastres as well as millièmes and keeping on (in its Egyptian version) the real or dollar, worth just over four shillings, which had been the main unit of pilgrim and tourist reckoning in Victorian times.

The kind of tourist who travelled with Cook's still had problems of another kind with money. Cook's warned him that *baksheesh* would probably be the first word he learned in the East and advised: "If each traveller would make it a rule never to give baksheesh except for some positive service rendered worth the sum given, he would confer a boon upon the people and upon future travellers."

Not all the travellers, however, were primarily concerned with seeing the sights and the antiquities or linking a winter voyage up the Nile to a spring visit to Palestine to see the Eastern Churches' Easter services, the Muslim festivals of Nebi Musa (soon to become a focus for Arab political feelings) and the Jewish Passover. Father Meistermann, for example, moved straight from his account of the Egyptian and proposed Palestinian coinages to an explanation of indulgences, including those attached to "souvenirs of the Holy Places". In his guide-book he marked places that rated a plenary indulgence with a Maltese cross and those to which a partial indulgence attached with a Latin cross. All these indulgences, he said, might be applied to the souls in Purgatory. Although cultural relations were closer, Roman Catholic and Protestant theological approaches to pilgrimage and holy places remained much where they were in the days of Bonar and McCheyne.

But there were two new emphases in the new situation of Palestine which drew travellers of very different kinds - pilgrims of a sort - and very strong opinions. One was an understandable anxiety among Jews and others to observe the development of the national home, often with a special emphasis on its socialist and even utopian experiments. The other was a revival of Christian, especially Protestant evangelical interest in Jewish missions. It differed, however, in many respects from the approach of Bonar and McCheyne or the English mission in the days of the Hebrew Bishop Alexander. Its hopes rested less on persuading orthodox Jews to see Old Testament passages in a new light than on hoping that Zionist Jews, many of them at odds with their religious traditions, would find that secularism was not enough, and that Christ was the Light of the World.

David Torrance's biographer W.P. Livingstone reflected
this mood when he reported a feeling that Jews "were groping
after a truer and more liberal interpretation of spiritual
verities".

Unfortunately those travellers to Palestine whose primary concern was with secular hope or divine favour often found
themselves reporting on the conflict which began in the
earliest stages of the Mandate and continued, with variations
and changes of direction, until its end, when Britain set down
the burden. If either the British or the Zionists were ignorant
in 1917 of the possible strength of Arab hostility they knew
better by the early 1920s. Harry Luke, for example, must have
found himself revising Cook's guide at the same time as he was
a commissioner inquiring into the causes of a clash in Jaffa
which cost nearly 100 lives.

When the medical missionary Alexander Paterson returned from Scotland to Hebron early in 1920 the first vivid
impression made on him was of the snow that covered great
tracts of the Judean uplands. There had been nothing in
Palestine in living memory like this snowfall, which stranded
carriages and travellers in vast drifts between Jerusalem and
Hebron and was followed by hailstones "the size of walnuts".
Dr Paterson remembered the rout of the Amorites (Joshua
10.12) when more were slain by hailstones than by the sword
of Israel, and recorded that "the Holy Land has always held its
own in the matter of climatic wonders."

But Paterson's second vivid impression was of the new
intensity of feeling against Zionism, which in practice meant
against the Jews. He reached Hebron through the snow-
covered hills on the same day that, far to the north, Captain
Joseph Trumpeldor, late of the Russian Army and the Zion
Mule Corps, was killed defending Jewish settlements against
Arab attacks. Around Hebron there were caches of arms laid
down by Arabs who had contrived to gather both German
and British rifles. Merchants who feared the troubles ahead
were selling off their stocks at reduced prices and calling in
their debts. Paterson himself was asked to join in street patrols
in the hope that his influence on the Arabs would help deter
a threatened attack on the Jewish quarter. Paterson, who took
an old-fashioned paternalistic view, wrote of the "Arab rab-

ble" who had proclaimed Feisal in Jerusalem as king of a Greater Syria and feared that Palestinian Christians would soon be ground between the millstones of Islamic fanaticism and Zionism.

He claimed that the Arabs eagerly welcomed the prospect of British suzerainty but that the Balfour Declaration "roused their fears, inflamed their passions, and quickened racial prejudice and antagonism".

In Tiberias another Scots medical missionary, D.W. Torrance, noted that 10,000 Jews had arrived in six months and (in his biographer's words) that "Palestine was beginning to throb with life in a way it had not known for centuries", with even some of the older Jewish inhabitants "dazed by what was going on".

In more than one respect David Watt Torrance, who had not long to live, combined prophetic vision with shrewd judgment as well as the practical good works of his hospital. His fame spread not only among the Jews, Muslims, and Christians of Galilee and elsewhere in Palestine but far beyond the Jordan, and he was both affectionately and respectfully known as the "Hakim of Tiberias". But he also saw in the new wave of well educated, skilled, hard-working, and mainly East European Jewish immigrants - the *halutzim* or pioneers - the "nucleus of the future commonwealth of the Jews". He defended them against the charge of "Bolshevism" in a judgment that later events in the Soviet Union were to justify. "These Jews, however revolutionary their ideas are in regard to orthodox Judaism, are loyal to their race and their aim is national reconstruction and not the abolition of orderly society." The heirs of the Bolsheviks were in time to be bitter enemies of Zionism. But where even Torrance, like many pro-Zionist Christians, allowed good intentions and high hopes to take precedence over realistic judgment was in his view that but for extreme Zionists who wished "to create a Jewish State at once and by sheer force" the Arabs of Palestine would not have resented the new direction in which Palestine was moving.

The extremist Jews whom Torrance had in mind included those - later to break with the mainstream of political Zionism - like Vladimir Jabotinsky, spiritual father of Menachem

Begin. Jabotinsky not only proclaimed a "revisionist" demand for the colonisation of Palestine by millions of Jews but defined the country as a territory "whose chief geographical feature is this: that the River Jordan does not delineate its frontier but flows through its centre." It was a militant tendency that was to bring much bitterness to the later years of the British Mandate, through the Irgun Zwai Leumi and the "Stern Gang", and afterwards to set its mark on the structure of Israeli politics.

A few years after David Torrance's reflections on extremism and Bolshevism, his son and succesor in Galilee, Herbert Torrance, was to find some consolation in the way that only Tiberias of the four "holy cities" kept the peace when bloody Arab-Jewish clashes in Jerusalem were followed by attacks on Jews in Safed and Hebron. About 100 on each side were killed in that flare-up of 1929, most of the Jews by the Arabs and most of the Arabs by the British-organised police. The Mandate was already becoming a burden rather than an enlightened imperial opportunity.

It had begun rich in high hopes as well as good intentions, with Herbert Samuel as the first British High Commissioner. Samuel was a Jew, which ensured both his unpopularity with the Arabs and perhaps a determination on occasions to go out of his way not to seem biased in favour of the Zionists, who probably resented some of his decisions even more than if they had come from a British Gentile. He tried hard to be fair but this was a situation in which (to quote the historian Christopher Sykes) "fairness could be of no avail".

Among Samuel's guests in 1921 was one of the most eminent of all British visitors to Jerusalem and imperial rulers of the Holy Land, a former colleague in Asquith's Cabinet. By then Winston Churchill was Colonial Secretary in Lloyd George's Coalition Government. He had responsibility for Mandated territories, including Palestine, and and was especially anxious to settle the affairs of Transjordan with its emir-designate and future king Abdullah, son of the Sherif of Mecca and brother of Feisal. As might have been expected, it was an eloquent visit: for example at a military cemetery dedication on the Mount of Olives Churchill spoke of those who fell in 1917 lying "here where rests the dust of the Khalifs, the

Crusaders, and the Maccabees". But it was also a troubled one. The Jews, who rightly regarded Churchill as well-disposed, feared that he would yield ground to the intensity of Arab feeling which was both organised for him and expressed to him.

On that occasion they need not have worried. It demonstrated an early example not only of the assertion of Arab Palestinian nationality but of the way that Muslim misjudgment of the West, fanaticism, and rhetorical exaggeration over-stated the legitimate Arab case. The Arabs demanded the abandonment of the Balfour Declaration, which was both politically and morally impossible for the British Government now that it was part of the terms of the Mandate. Their memorandum to Churchill was not only anti-Zionist but anti-Jewish, claiming that the Jew "encourages wars when self-interest dictates, and thus uses the armies of the nations to do his bidding". It showed how out of touch the Arabs were with the trends of Jewish life in Palestine when they wrote off Hebrew (now an official language there) as "a dead language". It tried unskilfully to exploit Western fears that Bolshevism was largely Jewish and used language about the role of Jews in the German and Austrian collapse of the kind which later became part of Nazi mythology. Zionists not only wanted to establish a Jewish State in Palestine but gradually "to control the world". Arab policy was ill-directed and ill-expressed long before its most outspoken leader, Haj Amin El Husseini, whom Samuel approved as Mufti of Jerusalem in 1921, achieved his later notoriety as an ally of Hitler.

Not suprisingly, the moderately pro-Zionist Churchill replied that he had no power to reverse British policy and would not do so if he had, and was drawn into reminding the Arabs that it was not they but the British who had overthrown Turkish rule. The national home was "one of the facts definitely established by the triumphant conclusion of the Great War".

Churchill also visited Tel Aviv and, at the urging of Chaim Weizmann, the nearby pioneer settlement of Bir Yaakov where the road-building Jewish immigrants assured him they were not Bolsheviks but dedicated to the ideals of labour and building the national home through self-help and physical exertion. The interpreter and guide was Pinhas Rutenberg, an engineer and enthusiast of drive and genius who 'had left Russia when Kerensky's Government was overthrown by the Bolsheviks. He then surveyed Palestine's water supplies, established the electricity company which helped transform the country, and became one of the leading Jewish advocates of co-operation with the Arabs.

Later at Rishon-le-Zion, not far from where Herzl had once led Zionist children in singing the Kaiser's praises, Churchill too was met by "admirable children" and "white-clothed damsels". He was then invited (as he also told the House of Commons) "to sample the excellent wines which the establishment produced" - and which years before George Adam Smith had taken for his stomach's sake. The biographer Martin Gilbert (a British Jewish sympathiser with Zionism) notes that the visit increased Churchill's sympathy with the national home, but his narrative inevitably reveals how even a generous, dynamic, and fair-minded Englishman was being drawn still farther into the mixture of ambiguities and illusions created by the declaration of Balfour, the philosophic Scotsman. For the grandest of the illusions was the hope that the progress of the national home - which Churchill described eloquently to Parliament - would create a Palestine of progress and prosperity in which the Arabs would both share and appreciate the benefits of Jewish achievement. In fact the progress of the national home, at a time when nationalism was spreading and growing in intensity throughout the Middle East, only made it more certain that there would be an all-out conflict of Jews and Arabs if ever British authority were relaxed or withdrawn.

Only a strong, consistent British policy sustained over a long period could have made the most of whatever chance there was for peaceful progress in Palestine while the national home was built under its authority and protection. Samuel, for example, expected the Mandate Government to last "for many years", although it would gradually employ more local officials to take over from Britons. But British policy became visibly hesitant and uncertain. Even Samuel found himself suspending Jewish immigration at one stage of acute tension. That policy also had to be shaped in a world far less peaceful and stable than the peacemakers of 1919 had hoped for. Palestine had enough troubles of its own, but its future was dramatically influenced, especially after Hitler's triumph in 1933, by the troubles and evils of Europe.

Before 1933 the progress of the national home had been considerable but less spectacular than had seemed likely in the first flush and rush after the Balfour Declaration and the end of the war. In the 1920s most German, as well as British, American, and French Jews expected to stay in the country where they felt at home and increasingly integrated. Some German Jews had mixed feelings about a national home which was part of a peace settlement imposed by those against whom they had fought. They had their share of Iron Crosses, and a future president of the World Jewish Congress, Nahum Goldman, had worked as a German propagandist during the war. Even when anti-Semitism grew in Poland or Hungary (as it did well before the collapse of the Weimar Republic in Germany) the attractiveness of Palestine fluctuated. One of the main influences was the condition of the Jews in Poland; the other was economic conditions in Palestine itself. There were 14,000 Jewish immigrants in 1926 and only 3000 in 1927, when more Jews left Palestine than came in. But a strong tide of immigration flowed in from 1932, the years before Hitler came to power, and there were were 65,000 new Jewish arrivals in 1935.

The rise of Hitler had alarmed Jews. His coming to power in 1933 began to displace them from Germany, though the tremors spread to other countries. Even after Hitler began his persecution only about 12 per cent of Jewish immigrants to Palestine were German refugees, though others came from his Austrian homeland. By far the largest group of immigrants still came from Poland.

At the time it seemed that the refugees from Germany were the least fortunate of their people and that the immigrants from East Central Europe were taking more risks than the relatives they left behind. Later events showed that they were those who escaped in time from a still more terrible ordeal.

# 11  AN APPROACHING DISASTER

*THROUGH WORLD WAR TO CIVIL WAR*

The rise of Hitler destroyed the last hope of keeping the conflict in Palestine under control and waiting to see where gradualism would lead. There was a new enthusiasm as well as eventually a new necessity in Jewish immigration, and a new urgency too in Arab resistance to it. But that urgency, aiming to check Jewish immigration before the national home was powerful enough to seek statehood in at least part of Palestine, took three very different forms. The more radical Arabs moved from sporadic violence to the guerrilla warfare which the British called "the Arab Rebellion". Their leaders included the Grand Mufti of Jerusalem who was later to spend the war years in Germany, and they intrigued with those who seemed likely to be Britain's enemies. More cautious or conservative Arabs on better terms with the British played on anxieties about the need for friendship with the Muslim world in the difficult times ahead.

British emotions and policies were alike confused. Among officials and soldiers there was a shift of sympathy from Zionism and the Jews - who often seemed clever, pushing, and brusque - towards the easy-paced dignity of the more traditional Arabs. Even the Mufti kept up appearances until his flight to Syria to avoid arrest and was ready to conduct distinguished visitors round the Temple Mount, though the well connected young scholar Steven Runciman found him "over-affable". In high political places the romanticism of the Lloyd George, Churchill, and Balfour approach gave way for the moment to a new pragmatism which was often timid and cautious. It hoped, in the best sense of a word which had not yet been debased, for appeasement. But just as appeasement in wider international affairs came to mean deferring to the arrogance of aggressive dictators, appeasement of the conflict in Palestine came to mean giving ground in face of Arab pressure.

The Balfour Declaration was never actually rescinded in theory but British policy seemed to be moving towards a ban on further Jewish immigration at precisely the moment when Palestine seemed to offer the main hope for large numbers of European Jews. The awkward question of resolving the inherent contradiction of the Balfour Declaration was being aproached by a policy of not allowing the Jews to become a majority in Palestine or even a large enough minority to turn the national home into a Jewish State. The High Commissioner most associated with this trend (though political responsibility rested with the Ramsay MacDonald and Baldwin Governments) was Sir Arthur Wauchope, an upright and tenacious former soldier who became one of the first elders of the new Scots kirk in Jerusalem. His moves towards the creation of a legislative council - the pattern for a future Palestine Parliament - inevitably increased the tension between Jews and Arabs.

Yet this same British pragmatism inevitably led to the first tentative plans for a future partition of the Holy Land and the unavoidable difficulties about the status of Jerusalem, sacred to three religions, politically fiercely contested, and yet (as Bonar and McCheyne had recognised back in 1839) "the centre of the Jewish world". But the partition plans ran up against the problem that it was virtually impossible to delineate even a small Jewish State which would not have a very large Arab minority. For example the Peel Commission of 1937 proposed a Jewish area on the coast and in Galilee which (as the populations stood at the time) would have 258,000 Jews and 225,000 Arabs but excluded the Jewish majority in Jerusalem. The 1939 White Paper of Malcolm MacDonald (son of Ramsay) bowed to Arab pressure and seemed to Zionists to be the great betrayal. It envisaged that Jews should be about a third of Palestine's population and that after the admission of 75,000 immigrants in five years further admissions should depend on Arab approval - which meant a ban on immigration.

One result of this political confusion and bitterness is that much of the "literature" of Mandate Palestine in English is a

mixture of polemic, propaganda, and official report. "Of the
making of books about Palestine there is no end", wrote the
evangelical Christian J.W. Clapham; but many of them were
political and sociological treatises, often more concerned with
collectivist experiments than the religious or even national
significance of the Jewish return to the Land. The temper of
the times ensured that probably disproportionate attention
was devoted to the collective *kibbutzim*, especially those of
them that seemed to have all but eliminated family life, at the
expense of the co-operative *moshavim*, the older smallholding
colonies of *moshavot*, and even the development of commerce
and industry in Tel Aviv and Jerusalem.

Yet the older appeal of the Holy Land and the mixture of
danger and excitement in its new era could still stir some
worth-while travellers' tales. The best-selling H.V. Morton
was probably at his best with *In the Steps of the Master* and the
Ulster playwright St John Ervine wrote a lively sceptical book
about the Holy Places. His *Journey to Jerusalem* was in the
Mark Twain tradition. Even the political pilgrims sometimes
responded to the occasion, like the British Jewish writer
Maurice Pearlman. When Pearlman took a bus journey from
Netanya to Hedera a few days after his arrival in 1936 it was
lucky for him that he was so struck by an interesting village
on the way that he made an unscheduled break in his journey.
The bus went on without him and the passenger who took his
seat on this stretch of the coast road, halfway between Tel
Aviv and Haifa, was killed by an Arab bomb. "It prepared me
for the rest of my stay", he wrote, and his sociological travel-
book began to read like a manual of defensive infantry tactics
- as well as a compendium of contemporary Jewish com-
plaints, including one that the British troops "had orders not
to be too energetic".

In the early stages of the Arab Rebellion British policy had
certainly been indecisive. Wauchope, whose policy appeared
pro-Arab to the Zionists, seemed to the Arabs far too friendly
to the Jews. He was said to love every stone in Palestine and
to have given away much of his personal fortune in benefac-
tions there. But he was reluctant to accept how deep and
irreconcilable the conflict had become, to resort to martial
law, and to use the army to overawe the Arabs or forestall

guerrilla attacks. The Palestine Police too, despite their later reputation for toughness, had more doves than hawks. In the first stages of the rebellion in 1936 the scale of the problem also seems to have presented difficulties to the army and the police, who had only a few hundred Britons in a mixed force. In those days before large-scale air transport troop movements depended on the speed of troopships and trains, and it took time even to send reinforcements from Egypt.

The result was that some visitors to Palestine, including students, found themselves hurriedly enrolled along with British and other European residents in a kind of emergency home guard or volunteer auxiliary police to be used for guarding vulnerable sites. Among them was Tom Torrance, a gifted young Scots theology student who had a study fellowship and was a distant relative of the Tiberias Torrances. Some of his fellow-students were too pacifist to volunteer, but he diversified his study of biblical languages and archaeology with a stint on security duties. His first job was to protect vulnerable oil installations overlooking the "German colony" area not far from the Scots church in Jerusalem. His next was to stand guard along with a Dutchman over Barclay's Bank, which housed such treasures as the Emperor of Ethiopia had been able to retain in his flight from the invading Italians.

"The only trouble we had was with a small bomb flung at the door of the bank", he said. But trouble was to follow when he visited Petra and other parts of Transjordan, and at Kerak he was hauled up before a police chief who wanted his views on Hitler. Young men in khaki shirt and shorts were assumed to be Jewish, though in Amman Torrance added an Arab head-dress to his outfit. His troubles included something very nasty in the coffee and an incident "when a Bedouin the driver of my taxi picked up drew a revolver on me hissing the word *Yahudi*". But he got back safely to Jerusalem.

In spite of warnings he left again to tour northern Palestine and go over the border. "Somehow my brief association with the Palestine Police followed me, and the excuse it provided for Arab enmity against me, even when I crossed into Syria and Lebanon. The flames of anti-semitism were spreading everywhere." At one point, he remembers, "the Lord preserved me" when someone threw a knife that just missed his neck.

The trip that had taken Tom Torrance to Palmyra, Baalbek, and Sir Leonard Woolley's excavations in the Orontes valley carried on into Irak and Ur of the Chaldees, where he decided: "Since I had come so far, I thought I might as well visit Basra. Then my troubles began in earnest." From the train he saw Iraki planes bombing dissident Marsh Arabs and at Basra the Indian postmaster warned him he was in for trouble "and pointed me to a number of people hanging dead by the neck, accused of being Jews who had been stirring up trouble. Martial law had been declared. He had hardly ceased talking when I was arrested and taken away to the C.I.D. headquarters. Someone had apparently told them of my activities in Jerusalem in helping the British police."

Torrance was brought before a court of civilian and military police, accused of being a Jewish instigator of rebellion, and denied access to the British consul who could confirm who he was. He explained he was planning to visit the ancient Babylon on his way back to Baghdad. "But they would have none of it and formally condemned me to death. I shall never forget that moment. I saw the dead men hanging by the neck, thought of my dear mother, and prayed."

Fortunately for later Christian theology (and not least the exploration of harmonies in religious and scientific thought) the tribunal had second thoughts. Someone put in a telephone call. There was a discussion which Torrance's Arabic wasn't good enough to follow. He was told he was free to go - only to be accosted promptly by an Iraki who claimed to be a failed Edinburgh medical student and joined by another who was (or said he was) an Oxford graduate. There were curious conversations about the geography of the medical buildings in Edinburgh and about a conference on China sponsored by the Master of Balliol which Torrance had attended. When he tried to slip away it turned out the police had been watching and he found himself back at headquarters, but this time sentenced to be sent to Baghdad rather than to be hanged. Nevertheless he allowed himself a last request: to be allowed off the train at Hillah to photograph the ruins of Babylon. He managed it, only to have the photographs seized before his deportation to Damascus.

His troubles were not quite over. At Damascus he found an Hotel de Paris which looked European in style and had clean sheets, though the management were rather surprised when he insisted that he was alone. The next day he went to a service at the Edinburgh Medical Missionary Society's hospital chapel and caused consternation when he gave his temporary address. "Apparently the Hotel de Paris was a high-class brothel." The matron told him he was too young to be travelling alone, arranged a car to rescue his belongings, and ensured he slept that night in a ward bed - which was just as well, for he was about to be hit by a raging week of sand-fly fever, with which the hospital was better equipped to cope than the Hotel de Paris.

At the other end of the Damascus Road which St Paul had travelled, the first fury of the Arab Rebellion had died down and both sides prepared for a long conflict in which guerrilla war and political pressure both played their part. If the Palestinian administration tended to be slighly pro-Arab, and the army command tried to be impartial as well as cautious, there were other British residents, visitors and even soldiers who were very pro-Jewish indeeed. For example there is some irony in Maurice Pearlman's complaint about the army not being "energetic enough" when one studies his itinerary and the later course of events at one of the settlements he visited, Ein Harod in the Valley of Esdraelon near Mount Gilboa. The *kibbutz* was close to the waters where Gideon had once collected his troops to fight the Midianites and used the curious personnel selection procedures described in the Book of Judges (7.5), picking 300 men who drank "as a dog laps"; and a new Gideon was soon to be at hand.

Orde Wingate is best remembered now outside Israel for the Chindit campaigns in Burma. He was also a Christian Zionist of Scots ancestry. His father was an Indian Army colonel who had taken up with the Plymouth Brethren but his grandfather had served with "Rabbi" Duncan at the Scots mission to the Jews of Budapest, founded when the two older colleagues of Bonar and McCheyne came home by the Danube route.

Wingate could be described according to taste as a controversial enthusiast or a headstrong fanatic, in military matters as well as spiritual ones. In the mid-1930's he was a Gunner captain qualified as an Arabic specialist but too committed to the Zionist cause to be considered dependable in staff and intelligence work. His immediate superiors complained that he was giving political advice to the Zionists and, in the words of a friendly field-marshal, Lord Ironside, "he got a black mark for being too Jewish". But he had been allowed to develop his own tactics and show his powers of leadership in defending Jewish settlements against Arab attack, creating mixed squads of British soldiers and men from the *kibbutz* to ambush Arab infiltrators.

He also added a curious footnote to the English literature of the Holy Land: a fifteen-page "complaint to the Sovereign" protesting against an adverse confidential report. This ponderous appeal procedure under the Army Act failed in theory but in fact Wingate won a kind of draw. He was barred from involving himelf again in Palestinian affairs, even by the sympathetic General Wavell, but was picked out by his admirers in high places for future opportunities, making his mark (and still more enemies) until his death in an air crash during the second Chindit expedition. Wingate takes a notable place among the military pilgrims on the road to Zion, as distinctive and at times wayward in this century as General Gordon had been in the previous one.

Wingate was a loner, but by no means alone among evangelical Christians in his enthusiasm for the Jewish cause in Palestine. But missionary civilians had not his soldier's advantage of being able to find an immediate common cause and purpose with the most fervent Zionists. They worked, prayed, and pondered on the significance of the Jewish return. To read the inter-war reports of "Jewish missions" is to encounter a mood in which excitment and frustration mingle and are sometimes flavoured by a good deal of self-deception. It was disconcerting to discover how secular and even atheist some of the Zionists had become, but even in that loss of belief Evangelicals thought they might find a divine purpose. The

decay of traditional Jewish faith and observance would surely
create a spiritual vacuum which Hebrew Christianity would
eventually fill.

A handful of the Evangelicals passionately concerned
about the Jews and therefore the national home were themselves Hebrew Christians, like the Safed-born Sir Leon Levison
(brother of Nahum) who revisited his home town in 1930, met
his mother and others of his family, and later added to a note
of his suprise at the extent of his welcome: "The thing that
cheered my heart most was the numerous callers who sought
me in private to discuss religion". Reconciliation had been
encouraged by the support which the International Hebrew
Christian Alliance (of which Levison was president) had
shown to the Jews after the Arab attacks at Safed and elsewhere in 1929.

A dispassionate view with the benefit of hindsight, however, suggests that even the limited successes achieved by the
Hebrew Christian movement tended to be among the Jews
integrated in European society and not those who emigrated
to Palestine. Attempts to establish a major Hebrew Christian
colony came to nothing. The verdict of Levison's son and
biographer is reasonable: "The most that can be said is that in
the post-war years a few pockets of Hebrew Chrtistianity are
to be found in Israel", and that even the later "Israeli Government clampdown on proselytising" has not stifled missionary
witness. Nor of course has it prevented the emergence of the
"Messianic Jews" with a different style and American connections to establish an authentic but awkward place both in
Israeli life and the Christian world.

But some of the Evangelicals who were encouraged by
what proved exaggerated hopes still proved to be shrewd
observers and witnesses to the course of history in the Holy
Land. For example J.W. Clapham's book *Palestine: The Land
of my Adoption*, published during the Second World War, is a
useful chronicle both of Evangelical hopes and Jewish attitudes, as well as of the way the Arab riots and revolt checked
the "effervescence and exuberance" of the early Mandate
years.

Clapham was one of those claiming to find an increasing
demand for the New Testament among Palestinian Jews and

that Jews were "beginning to wonder or even believe". Almost
every missionary since modern Jewish missions began made
similar claims at some stage, and not least those who worked
in the Holy Land. But it is credible that Clapham found a
section of the Jewish community ready to accept Jesus as a
great reformer, especially when the evangelist occasionally
reports phrases from civil but bluntly-spoken arguments with
Jews he met in Tiberias restaurants or on his travels - phrases
that seem to capture a mood of the time:

> My Gospel is the gospel of hard work. I have no
> other.... The Messiah we are looking for is freedom
> and equality among men.

But Clapham ended his book with a vision of Armageddon
and "the time of Jacob's trouble" before the Second Coming
to the Mount of Olives. "The severest trial both for the Jewish
people and the Gentile nations still lies ahead."

In fact there came a whole series of tribulations. The Jews
of Palestine agonised over the fate of their people trapped in
wartime Europe and fretted over the halt to immigration.
They had no doubt who had to win the world conflict, while
the Arabs waited to see who was going to win. Despite
continuing political ferment, Palestine enjoyed a certain detachment and prosperity amid the anxiety of the earlier war
years, serving as something between a vast base-camp and a
rest camp. According to Steven Runciman (one of whose
wartime tasks was writing Palestine Radio's news bulletin
reporting the Japanese attack on Pearl Harbour) the atmosphere relaxed enough for him to invite professors at the
Hebrew University to meet socially with Arab intellectuals.
Tens of thousands of soldiers again found themselves going up
to Jerusalem as pilgrims in uniform while the war rumbled not
far from Palestine's frontiers.

A few of them, like John Connell in *The House by Herod's
Gate*, left minor but valuable literary memorials. One, Ronald
Brownrigg, went up to Mount Zion as a general staff officer
and found an inspiration which led him to become eventually
Dean of St George's Cathedral in Jerusalem and one of the
great authorities on post-war pilgrimage and the development
of group travel.

When Britain was hard-pressed in the Middle East in 1941 Palestine was the base for a sad, sharp little war with the Vichy French across the border in Lebanon and Syria. In 1942 it braced itself as Rommel's German-Italian army reached Alamein before being halted and turned back. And as the tide of the great war receded the preparations for resumption of the local war became inevitable. The Jewish extremist fringe began the campaign of assassination and sabotage that was later to draw the British Army as well as the police into a bitter and unwinnable war against terrorism in the last years of the Mandate. The Haganah, the Jewish defence force which had existed for years on a semi-public, semi-legal basis, became an underground army. The Arabs checked their weapons and looked across Palestine's borders to wonder what help would come if the British ever left. Soon it became a question not of whether the British would leave but when and how.

The saddest phase in the British connection with the Holy Land was about to begin, a time of arms-searches, murders, hangings, and bombings as well as a build-up to guerrilla war and the disintegration of law and order. The British war cemeteries and memorials of the Holy Land mark not only the victories of 1917-18 but soldiers and police killed in the Arab Rebellion and in the last phase of the Mandate, when most clashes were with Jewish extremists.

An insoluble security problem, with terrorism used on both sides as Arab attacks brought Jewish reprisals followed by counter-reprisals, drifted towards civil war. An insoluble diplomatic problem was compounded by a rift over Palestine between the Attlee Government in Britain and the Truman administration in Washington, which did not always know its own mind. The State Department worried both about Middle East oil and about the opportuntiy for the Soviet Union to exploit the Palestinian crisis. The main forum for argument and attempted compromise moved from Whitehall and Westminster to Washington and the newly created United Nations, which drew up its own plan for partition in 1947. This allotted the Jews substantial areas in both Northern and Southern Palestine with a thin coastal strip to link them but neither control of Jerusalem nor a corridor to it. The British Army awaited orders, had the unpleasant duty of turning

away illegal Jewish immigrants who had survived the Holocaust, separated the combatants as best it could for as long as
it could, and eventually concentrated on securing its own
communications, planning to evacuate from Haifa and into
Egypt. It intervened in many places to avert worse violence
and massacre but its patrols did not and probably could not
prevent Arab attacks on the Jewish convoys on which Jerusalem depended. Inevitably it was criticised both when it intervened and when it failed to intervene. It tried to do its job and
often hated its work.

Not many British soldiers remembered that time with
affection, and many returned with something far short of
affection for the contending parties. The terrorist war waged
by the Jewish extremists left a particular legacy of bitterness,
as did some of the counter-measures. For a short time Britain
was close to the kind of "dirty war" which the French were
later drawn into in Algeria.

The most literary, as well as the most sensitive and
understanding of the soldiers was Bernard Fergusson, who
had been seconded to be assistant inspector-general of the
Palestine Police, a Christian who (as he eloquently told me
years later) loved the land, hated terrorism, and respected both
Jewish and Arab points of view. As he wrote in his autobiography *The Trumpet in the Hall*, he felt guilty on Sundays if he
missed the Scots kirk and took the chance to fly north to go
sailing in the relative calm of Acre. But the Bible and hymn-
book still guided his meditations on the early morning flight
over the clear landscape. He wondered that the sluggish and
placid river Kishon below could turn to the spate that swept
away the enemies of Deborah and Barak as told in Judges 5;
and as he looked across to Galilee he thought wryly of
Whittier's verse about Sabbath rest and calm, and the silence
of eternity interpreted by love. "There was no love whatever
about the place: only implacable hate."

By March 1948 there was a full-scale civil war in
Palestine, though the presence of the British Army deterred
the overt intervention of neighbouring States. It had to stay on
until the formal end of the British Mandate, due on May 15.

Not many Christian pilgrims went up to Jerusalem in
those last sad weeks. One who did was the Moderator of the

Scots Kirk's General Assembly, Dr Matthew Stewart, who
was due to be in Palestine for Easter and visit three Scottish
battalions (Argylls, K.O.S.B and H.L.I.) accompanied by his
chaplain John Fraser, a Gordon Highlander of the First World
War and a future Moderator. Fraser left an account of this
agonising journey. At Rehovoth their train was held up, for
the Jews had blown up a bridge on line as a reprisal for
bombings in Jerusalem. Near Bir Yaakov, where Churchill
had once been assured the Jewish pioneers were not Bolsheviks, the Moderator watched in his lace and breeches while an
Arab raiding party tried to plunder the armoury at a British
military hospital. The Scots were due to visit the hospital but
a friendly Arab had stopped the convoy.

When, after going through a maze of road blocks in Haifa
and a relatively peaceful visit to Galilee, they eventually drove
up to Jerusalem by the Bab-el-Wad on Maundy Thursday
(March 25) they passed "the remains of a Jewish convoy
destroyed but an hour or so before". When they reached
Jerusalem they found it barricaded into security zones, with
British civilians already being evacuated amid a regular pound-
ing of mortars and rattle of machine-gun fire. The planned
Maundy Thursday procession from St Andrew's to
Gethsemane had to be cancelled, as Jews and Arabs were
exchanging small-arms fire across the route.

However Good Friday turned out to be the quietest day
since the U.N. partition plan was announced in November
and a procession of Arab Christians went along the Via
Dolorosa to the Church of the Holy Sepulchre, where the
approaches were guarded by the "Arab Liberation Army" in
checked red and white head-dresses. At St Andrew's Dr
Matthew Stewart preached to a congregation which included
many off-duty men of the H.L.I. A journalist present (J.L.
Hays of the Aberdeen Press and Journal) reported that "the
Jocks took their rifles to church with them and laid them
down in the aisles."

Food rationing had to be introduced in Jerusalem at
Easter. In the subsequent weeks the fighting became even
more bitter, especially after the massacre of Arab villagers at
Deir Yassin west of Jerusalem on April 9 by Irgun and Sternist
elements - an action for which the Jewish Premier-designate

David Ben Gurion apologised to King Abdullah of Jordan. In
the divided city Bertha Spafford Vester, who had seen to the
care of Deir Yassin orphans, drove from the American Colony in a bullet-proof car to say good-bye to Sir Alan
Cunningham, the last in the line of High Commissioners that
began with Herbert Samuel. She thought it was sad to see the
British go, despite their mistakes. "But I ask, which Govern-
ment could have done a better job?" Later she found that the
Anglicans had made a breach in the wall of the St George's
Cathedral close to provide a safer passage to the American
colony. Among those she met there was the chaplain of Christ
Church, once Bishop Alexander's cathedral. He had been
ordered to quit his untenable position just inside the Jaffa
Gate, and had still to await a safe opportunity to leave the city.
The close had been designated as the "rallying point" for the
Brtitish community.

On the other side of Jerusalem, not far above the Bethlehem road, was the Scots church and hospice. Its trouble was
not only the sniper fire, but the risk that it might be seized as
a good defensive position and observation post. St Andrew's,
looking across the Valley of Hinnom with a fine view of
Mount Zion, was a memorial dedicated in 1930 to the dead of
another war - the Scots who had died in Allenby's campaign.
Much of the momentum had come from Ninian Hill, an
Edinburgh shipowner and elder who became its first minister,
but whose plans at one stage had run into criticism, one of the
grounds being that a Scots minister would be out of place "in
the decadent atmosphere of modern Jerusalem". In these last
days of the Mandate the atmosphere was not so much decadent as explosive. St Andrew's was shaken by blast from the
shelling of the nearby Montefiore village and then exposed to
small-arms and mortar fire.

Its minister then was William Clark Kerr, a talented watercolour painter about whose later fortunes the records of the
Scots ministry are ominously silent. But in that terrible spring
of 1948 he kept the flag flying - quite literally. He stayed on to
claim possession and sought help where he could, trying to
persuade the Arab National Committee that seizure would be
bad public relations and inducing the British Army to send a
detachment to provide a brief interlude of protection even

during the preparations for evacuation. Then, on his own again, he reported back to Edinburgh: "All night battle round the building.... St Andrew's Cross on both church and manse. If that is not enough will try Rampant Lion."

As the battle raged and the kirk found itself on the Jewish edge of a no man's land, Clark Kerr continued to ring the bell and go through the service on Sundays. It was, he said, not only to continue tradition unbroken and let those within earshot know he was still alive. It was also "because I felt I could have communion not only with God but with all who were praying with us for this broken land."

So ended the British Mandate.

It ended ingloriously, reviled by both sides and with its limited achievements overshadowed by the conflict. But without it there would have been no State of Israel.

# 12   ISRAEL RESTORED, THE LAND DIVIDED

*"THE HOLOCAUST THAT IN OUR TIME DESTROYED MILLIONS OF JEWS IN EUROPE AGAIN PROVED BEYOND DOUBT THE COMPELLING NEED TO SOLVE THE PROBLEM OF JEWISH HOMELESSNESS AND DEPENDENCE BY THE RENEWAL OF THE JEWISH STATE IN THE LAND OF ISRAEL"*

*- FROM THE PROCLAMATION OF THE INDEPENDENCE OF ISRAEL, MAY 14, 1948.*

The "renewal of the Jewish State in the Land of Israel", proclaimed as the afternoon wore on towards the Sabbath eve, was timed to come into effect when the British Mandate formally ended at midnight. It claimed a natural and historic right, and the warrant of a United Nations resolution on November 29, 1947 calling for the establishment of a Jewish State in part of Palestine.

Politically and diplomatically May 15 was a watershed in the troubled history of Palestine as well as a day of profound significance in world and Jewish history, and for all travellers to the Holy Land. Once that independence had been claimed nothing in the Middle East could be the same again. Nor could relations between Israelis and their neighbours and between Jews and Christians. The right of Israel to recognition and survival inevitably became a matter of passionate concern to millions of Jews who had not been especially Zionist.

But the war that raged in Palestine even before the British departure intensified after the declaration of independence. In its later phases it radically changed the balance of population in the country and left a legacy of bitterness of which no pilgrim and traveller can be unaware. The Arabs who had

rejected the United Nations partition plan found themselves
in a far worse position than it had offered them. The war
created new controversies and human problems which nearly
50 years later have not been resolved.

The war which the Israelis call one for independence and
survival, and which the Arabs call one to defend and liberate
Palestine, was suspended by truce and not ended by peace. At
the time of writing only Egypt, of all the Arab countries which
came to help the Palestinians and co-ordinated their efforts so
badly, has made peace, though Jordan may long have awaited
a suitable moment.

The later visitor still encounters the consequences as well
as the controversies of the war of 1947-49. The main consequences are the distinction between "Israel proper" and the
areas variously labelled occupied territories, the West Bank
and Gaza, or Samaria and Judea. There are nuances in termi-
nology which often reflect the speaker's point of view.

In only one respect, the incorporation of East Jerusalem
(including the area within the historic walls) with the rest of
the city, does the Israel of the 1990s formally claim parts of
Palestine beyond the demarcation lines of 1949, even though
the Israeli victory in the Six-Day War of 1967 utterly changed
the terms of the provisional and precarious armistice lines of
1949. These themselves had put the Israelis in a better position
than they had occupied at the time of the first truces in 1948
not long before the murder (by Jewish extremists) of the
Swedish U.N. mediator, Count Folke Bernadotte. Between
the first two truces the Israelis captured Lydda and Ramleh,
and secured their hold on Nazareth, while the final round of
the War of Israeli Independence had important results away
from the main areas of pilgrim and tourist interest. It secured
the Jewish State the opportunity to develop the Negev desert.
However it also consolidated the Israeli position in Galilee
and on the coastal strip. The main limit to the Israeli success
(apart from the loss of the Jewish Quarter in the Old City of
Jerusalem) had been the defensive victory of the Arab Legion
on the main road to the Holy City from the coast, especially
at Latrun. As a result the Israelis had to drive a new road across
the Judean hills and live till 1967 with Jerusalem as the tip of
a vulnerable salient.

The most important and sensitive of the many controversies which still echo down the years is that of the Arab refugees, some of them refugees twice over after the 1967 war. Israeli propagandists will tell the visitor that those Arabs who could afford to left the areas where fighting was expected or in progress and that much larger numbers were encouraged to leave by their own leaders and allies, in the expectation that they would soon return. They point to areas, notably around Nazareth, where the Arabs stayed on and became Israeli citizens. Arabs and their sympathisers will say, picking up the idiom of the 1990s, that there was large-scale "ethnic cleansing", with various degrees of terror and intimidation used by the Israelis.

The pilgrim has neither the time nor the information to know where the truth lies, especially when historians as well as propagandists disagree, though he may note the verdict of Christopher Sykes. This historian suggested that most of the time in the first half of 1948 the mass exodus "was the natural, thoughtless pitiful movement of people who had been badly led" and who in the day of trial found themselves let down by their leaders. Terror was the impulse, by hearsay most often and sometimes through experience. He instanced as "experience" the looting of Jaffa, captured immediately before the proclamation of independence. But he also suggested that in the subsequent stages of the war, especially in Lydda and Ramleh, the exodus was "consciously and mercilessly helped on".

What seems beyond dispute is that about half the Arab population of Palestine was permanently displaced by the fighting. The Arab population of what became Israel in 1948 had been 650,000. When the fighting died away and some Arabs found their way back it was only 150,000, though there has since been a large natural increase. These are figures from the late Terence Prittie, a very fine Christian journalist sympathetic to the Israelis. Sykes gives higher figures, but similar in proportion. United Nations figures showed nearly a million people claiming to be refugees by 1950. Another U.N. figure of the time showed 750,000 people being fed by its relief agency. When all allowance is made for possible exaggeration, corruption, and the inclusion of some of the existing poor and unemployed in the area of U.N. relief operations, there is no disputing the enormous scale of the human disaster and misery which the war brought.

But however this great displacement of people happened, or was caused, 1948 brought not only a new State of Israel but a new face for the Land of Israel. Haifa, Lydda, and Jaffa all became mainly Jewish. Jaffa, some parts cleared and tidied up, others taken over by North African or Oriental Jews, was absorbed in the sprawl of Tel Aviv. In some parts of the country Arabs could look across the barbed wire and see Israelis ploughing their old fields. Sir John Glubb, who shaped the Arab Legion which became the Jordanian Army, called this "the frontier of hate" and wrote poignantly of a village where the Arabs kept their homes but looked across the demarcation line to see Jews picking the fruit in their old orange groves. But in many areas of Israel the effects of large-scale immigration and industrialisation changed the landscape. The Arab flight and the refugee camps it created also changed the face of the land in places outside the territory won for Israel, for example near Jericho and Nablus and above all in the crowded Gaza Strip. It also changed the character of the the East Bank, the old Transjordan, and of the Lebanon.

It was not simply, as Arabs sometimes argued, a case of the Middle East paying the price for European persecution of the Jews. The Holocaust could no more be excluded from the proclamation of Israel's independence than from the emotions of its people. But, after the first great post-war wave of immigration by the survivors of East European Jewry, there came a different movement of population as Jews moved to the Land of Israel - or returned to it - from Damascus, Beirut, Baghdad, Cairo, Alexandria, and the Yemen.

The reasons for this exodus can be disputed, like those for the flight of Arab refugees, but the effect of the conflict was to encourage Oriental as well as East European Jews to see Israel as their secure homeland. Others came in large numbers from North Africa as French rule came to an end in Morocco and Algeria. Some Arab Governments harassed or even persecuted Jews; none, amid the wars and rumours of more wars, let them feel at home. The result is that nearly half a century after the proclamation Israel is not only a country of the Middle

East but a Jewish State with more Oriental Jews than Westerners. Immigration from Russia will not be enough to restore the
earlier domination by the Ashkenazim.

As always, most Christian pilgrims were relatively indifferent to the vexed politics of the Holy Land. But the most
non-political pilgrim encounters the consequences of the
Jewish-Arab quarrel and its aftermath. That remains true in
the 1990s, even in tourist-conscious Bethlehem, never mind in
Nablus and Hebron or - should any pilgrim seek traces of the
Philistines who gave Palestine its name - in Gaza. But between
the resumption of relatively normal travel and pilgrimage in
the early 1950's and the Israeli victory in the 1967 war there
was a distinctive and remarkable interlude in the tangled
history of Holy Land travel. It was caused partly by the way
the truce-lines had been drawn, on the basis of who held what
when the fighting stopped, and partly by what happened on
the Arab side. The remnant of Arab Palestine did not became
a second independent State in the Holy Land. A small part of
it, the crowded Gaza strip, was controlled by Egypt. The main
part had become the "West Bank" of the Kingdom of Jordan.
The Old City of Jerusalem had seen yet another army pass that
way - the British-trained Arab Legion which had now become
the Jordanian army.

The new State of Israel was cut off from many of the most
holy or historic Jewish sites as well as from the most important
of the Christian "holy places". The Christian pilgrims of the
time found that two States competed for their favours in the
Holy Land, and found that the aftermath of war had caused
many complications. By an irony of history the Israelis found
themselves in posession of most of the coastal land of the
Philistines, except for the Gaza area. But they were barred
from Shechem. Their old foothold and new settlements in and
around Hebron had been over-run. They had also been
forced, after a bitter siege, to surrender and evacuate the
Jewish quarter of the Old City of Jerusalem. With it went
access to the "place of wailing" or Western Wall. The Israelis
did hold the Arab Christian town of Nazareth, and the
Christian pilgrims could visit its various dubious sites. Pilgrims and tourists in Israel could also go to Galilee, though

parts of it were dominated, threatened, and sometimes bombarded from the Syrian Golan Heights beyond the lake.

But the Temple area, the Church of the Holy Sepulchre, the Via Dolorosa, the Mount of Olives, Bethlehem, and the part of the Jordan associated with Christ's baptism were under the precarious but tenacious rule of the young King Hussein of Jordan, grandson of Abdullah, the Emir whose installation Winston Churchill had ratified on his 1921 visit to Jerusalem. King Abdullah himself had paid the price of moderation in a world of extremism. In 1949 he was assassinated in the doorway of the Aksa Mosque while attending Friday prayers on the Temple Mount in Jerusalem. Hussein succeeded in 1952 after the unhappy reign of the mentally unstable Tellal.

At Easter and Christmas there was a special dispensation for the Christians. "Pilgrims who are in Israel at Christmas and Easter can obtain special permission to visit to Holy Places in Jordan (for a limited period) and return to Israel via the Mandelbaum Gate", said the 1965 edition of Dr Zev Vilnay's guide-book.

This was the age of the Mandelbaum Gate, named after the owner of a nearby building, the one link in these years between Israel and the Arab world as well as between the two parts of Jerusalem. But the extent of the Christmas and Easter special arrangements suggests how restricted was the access and how difficult the travel. Foreign pilgrims seeking to enter the Old City via the gate needed to secure a permit from the Israelis, given after application through their own consuls. But they also needed acknowledgment of the permit from the Jordanians, "who have never accorded it to anyone of the Jewish faith", said Dr Vilnay. Even Gentiles who got safely through the gate into the Old City and the Arab world beyond had problems if they wanted to return to Israel. Vilnay advised flying to Cyprus and getting a re-entry visa without difficulty from the Israeli consulate there.

American Gentiles also appear to have been subject to scrutiny to make sure that no American Jews slipped into Jordanian Jerusalem among them. The Lutheran writer Betty Hartman Wolf, wife of an Ohio minister and biblical archaeologist, and author of a pleasant and non-political 1967 book about the parts of the Holy Land which were then in Jordan,

warned Americans seeking a Jordanian visa that "because of
the tensions betwen Israel and Jordan tourists should be aware
of the fact that Jordanian officials may require them to show
a letter or document proving church membership".

It was possible for Christian pilgrims who had come to
Jordan to cross into Israel by the Mandelbaum Gate, but again
the procedure was cumbersome, for entry visas had to be
applied for, either before setting out at an Israeli consulate or
through the traveller's consulate in the Old City, a procedure
which usually took three days. In each case the visitor didn't
collect his visa in advance. He turned up at the Mandelbaum
gate and hoped it was waiting for him.

In practice it does not always seem to have been so
difficult, especially for those pilgrims who came in parties and
had tour organisers, well versed in the ways of the land and of
the world, to handle for them the formalities of permits and
visas. For example in 1958 a Scots minister who later himself
led many tours, James Currie, was one of a party led by the
Anglican clergyman and former Jerusalem general staff officer
Ronald Brownrigg, who two years before had planned the
first Inter-Church Travel Holy Land itineraries and later
wrote a very successful and valuable pilgrim's handbook.
Currie recorded that they flew from Blackbushe in Hampshire to Lod two weeks after Easter and then crossed into
Jordan to lodge in the Claridge Hotel on the Mount of Olives,
where the hosts were kind but the water supply was not
guaranteed. This was their base for the Old City and its
surroundings, including the walk from Jerusalem to Bethany.
Currie also recorded that this party walked from the Upper
Room to Gethsemane which, if his recollection was correct
and the room site was the traditional one, meant that they
were able to cross a truce line. Later the party went to Israeli
Galilee and Currie was able to visit the Scots hospice at
Tiberias.

But many visitors to Israel made do with a view of the Old
City from the various vantage points in Israeli hands. Bethlehem could be seen at a distance from the *kibbutz* of Ramat-
Rahel, which had remained in Israeli hands after fierce fighting in 1948.

Despite these difficulties travel and tourism flourished. Israel, having taken over and developed the main Palestinian airport at Lod - Lydda in its British days - was well placed to make the most of the post-war expansion of air travel. Eager though it was to attract Christian pilgrims, it had the basis for a thriving tourist industry in the enthusiasm of Jews everywhere, but especially in the United States, to see Israel and show solidarity with it, even if they had no plans to move there. Hotels in an American style, richer in comfort than in character, began to appear in West Jerusalem.

On the Jordanian side, a Government constantly beset with political and economic troubles tried to make the most of one of its few assets, its possession of most of the "holy places". East Jerusalem and the Mount of Olives also saw the rise of new hotels, with guaranteed water supplies for their guests. There were flights linking the international airports at Cairo and Beirut with the local Jerusalem airport out towards Ramallah, north of the city. David Roberts' romantic art of 1839 appeared on Jordanian tourist calendars as well as Israeli picture-postcards. "Jordan is the Holy Land", said the sensitive and compassionate but very pro-Arab British literary traveller Ethel Mannin in 1965. In writing about the Hashemite Kingdom of Jordan she found it natural to begin with Jerusalem and move on to Bethlehem and Nazareth. Unfortunately Nazareth was since partition "no longer in Jordan". Even Betty Wolf, whose interest was more exclusively religious, found it expedient to emphasise that Jordan was "the land of Jesus" and to make little use of the terms Palestine and Palestinian.

In Jerusalem Ethel Mannin found the Church of the Holy Sepulchre was "collapsing and heavily buttressed", with scaffolding everywhere inside. The Dome of the Rock had just been repaired and restored by the Jordanians. The Jaffa Gate was out of use, for it looked into no man's land, but there were tourist buses in the square in front of the Damascus Gate. But even that was close to a new kind of wall - "The Sniper's Wall" which the Jordanians claimed was to prevent Israelis finding targets from their posts in the shattered Notre Dame convent. There were similar fears and precautions on the other side, both in and around Israeli Jerusalem and in the countryside.

When Ethel Mannin, who even put "Israel" in quotation marks, went to Nablus during a tour by King Hussein she noted that the drive was for some distance in sight of the sea, although the coast-line was in "occupied territory". There is also a vivid account of the view of the coast in Sir John Glubb's memoirs of Jordan in peace, war, and turbulence. Another way of putting the point was that the coastal corridor of Israel linking Haifa and Galilee with Tel Aviv (and Jewish Jerusalem, a long way round) was only a few miles wide.

This was inevitably an age when travel-writers in Palestine, even when they ceased for the moment to be war correspondents, found it hard not to be political propagandists. The 1949 armistice had not ended the war, which continued to be waged by every diplomatic and political means. But it did confine the actual fighting to border clashes and raids, some of them small-scale battles rather than mere skirmishes, and to Arab infiltration attacks which the Israelis understandably thought of as terrorism.

The Six-Day War of 1967, when the crushing Israeli defeat of Egypt was succeeded by victory over Jordan and Syria, created a very different situation. Once again the Arabs demanded confrontation and encountered disaster, losing still more of what they had retained. Jerusalem was reunited under Israeli control. Bethlehem and Nazareth now fitted into the same Christian itinerary. Tension relaxed in the parts of Galilee dominated by the Golan Heights. Jordan lost most of its tourism and was soon to face a bitter internal conflict with its Palestinian radicals.

Israel breathed more easily. There was no longer a constant threat to Jerusalem's communications and no enemy looking down on the coast between Tel Aviv and Haifa, with even Lod airport within his artillery range. The Galileans had a respite from intermittent bombardment. The guerrilla bases were no longer close to some of Israel's most productive agricultural areas.

The Israelis also, with some justification, expected a new golden age of tourism and pilgrimage.

# 13  PILGRIMS AND TOURISTS

*CUSTOMS OF THE COUNTRY, ANCIENT AND MODERN*

The Six-Day War of 1967 gave Israel military and political control of all Palestine, even if it did not solve the problems of a hostile and resentful Arab population. This time most of the Arabs did not flee, though many refugees and political activists did. They generally stayed put - first shocked, then sullen, later rebellious - even when the Israelis sprinkled settlements over parts of the West Bank and Gaza, and expanded into East Jerusalem.

One result of the Israeli conquest was a decisive victory in the battle for pilgrims and tourists. Probably more Christian visitors have come to the Holy Land in the last 25 years than at any other time in history, except possibly for the special circumstances of 1917-18 and 1939-45. And for the first time in the Christian era a Jewish Government controlled access to the Holy Land and its holy places and a Jewish society and public opinion had the main role in determining the customs of the country to which visitors had on occasion to conform. Tel Aviv may seem a secular city but the Sabbath draws in like a curtain early on Friday evening. The West Jerusalem hotels offer every modern comfort but the visitor may encounter odd gaps and patterns in the menu which a glance at the Book of Leviticus may make more understandable.

It was now Jordan (reduced to the old boundaries of Transjordan) that was isolated from the main stream of tourism. The airport at Lod - or Lydda - now provided as standard a pattern of entry to the Holy Land as the choppy approach on the breakers at Jaffa had done in earlier centuries. The pattern was relatively little changed when, from the end of the 1970's, the Begin-Sadat settlement made travel possible again between Israel and Egypt. The Israelis gave up their control of Sinai, where some tourism had developed, but they

retained their blue-water, blue-sky winter resort of Eilat at the
head of the Gulf of Akaba and saw the first tourism since 1939
to include the Pyramids and Jerusalem on the same itinerary.
But the day still seemed distant when travel agents could offer
a modern air-conditioned Grand Middle Eastern coach tour
taking in Damascus and Beirut, even Baghdad, as well as
Jerusalem and Cairo. Yet in some ways the isolation of Israel,
apart from the limited contacts with Egypt, fitted in well with
the economics of relatively cheap, direct flights and compact
tours on short holidays.

The country was in many ways isolated from its neighbours, but not from the Western world; and it was no longer
partitioned, at least for the pilgrim's principal purposes.
Jerusalem was one city again for tourists even before the
Israelis proceeded to the formal (though disputed) incorporation of the eastern part of the city. The Western or Wailing
Wall was not only accessible to all - virtually all Christian as
well as Jewish pilgrims went there - but given a new space and
dignity by the controversial clearance of its approaches, where
houses had formerly come within four metres of the wall. The
devastated Jewish Quarter of the Old City was restored and
given a splendour it had scarcely known before the battle in
1948.

For the Christian visitor Bethlehem was just down the
road, and a good place to go by Arab bus on the Sabbath. It was
under occupation but the Christian Arabs were both friendly
and hospitable to the pilgrim-tourist and Israeli troops around
Manger Square could be relatively relaxed. Galilee was accessible in reasonable security by taking the road down to
Jericho, past the Inn of the Good Samaritan and the abandoned Jordanian tank and then up the Jordan Valley. It was
safe and even relaxed to sail across from Tiberias and try the
fish at the settlement restaurant of Ein Gev, where the first
Jewish fishermen of modern times on the Sea of Galilee had
cast their nets. Nablus might not be recommended and
Hebron called for care - but that had been the pattern in
Victorian times and even during the Mandate.

Israel vigorously promoted tourism for economic as well
as ideological reasons, though (at least in the years immediately after the Six-Day War) the two still mingled. When I visited

Israel in 1974 on a Government-organised tour, designed to stimulate the interest of Christian editors in pilgrimage-tourism, the itinerary was a curious one for the purpose. The Temple Mount was scrupulously avoided and the Dome of the Rock seen only from afar, as Christian travellers had seen it in the days before the Turkish change of policy at the time of the Crimean War.

We had a brief stop in Nazareth - where a local Arab guide contrived a monumentally misjudged piece of flattery by assuring me, as he accepted his fee: "I know, sir, that you are English. You speak with the real English accent." But the crowded itinerary did not include Bethlehem, for it had to fit in the long journey down to the Dead Sea and then up to the fortress of Masada, with its emphasis on the Jewish defence to the last against the Romans. When it took us to Galilee it was to stay at an elegant kibbutz guest-house where the other visitors (apart from off-duty troops from the Lebanese frontier and Golan Heights) seemed to be bilingual in New York English and Yiddish. Courtesy required that we listened to an exposition of the aims and customs of the collective community, not all of them in line with the private-enterprise enthusiasm of the New Yorkers. Going to and from Galilee we kept well clear of Nablus and only skirted Samaria.

At Tiberias I had to beg a few minutes' stop to look in at the Scots hospice, once the Torrances' medical mission. In the Jordan valley the emphasis was on the archaeology of old Jericho, and we left the modern Arab town almost unvisited, as well as the now much depopulated refugee camps in the valley. Farther north, where the Jewish territory began, the memory of bombardment and shelters was still fresh and acute. And when we were allowed a free day before going home it was in Tel Aviv, admittedly only a bus ride from the Christian associations and institutions of Jaffa. It was exciting to hear a Russian-born Israeli speak of listening to Trotsky in the way that old men at home might speak of hearing Lloyd George, but those are not the excitements for which Christians come to the Holy Land.

But what of the Israeli who said of President Sadat - it was the time Henry Kissinger had achieved disengagement in Sinai after the Suez Canal fighting: "That Egyptian must be a very brave man"? There are times when even modern Israelis seem to have the insights of biblical times.

These few days gave me an insight into the difficulty which anyone in authority in the Holy Land can have in fully understanding the approach of others involved in it - even when (as in this case) the Israeli Government had both a sympathetic and an economic interest in encouraging Christian pilgrimage.

A few years later, at the jubilee celebrations for St Andrew's Scots Kirk, I encountered another part of the story. It was possible to be in the Holy Land, to walk around Jerusalem as Bartlett and Norman Macleod had done, to use the good offices and good contacts of Jerusalem's best Armenian Christian guide to tour the Haram, and yet be almost totally insulated from the interests and divisions of the country's people. One may return with such rare but incongruous memories as the sound of Highland pipes in the still evening air above the Valley of Hinnom. One may even be entertained by hospitable Arab Christians in Jerusalem or Bethlehem and hear little of the political anxieties around them and which they share.

It is this phenomenon of detachment which has produced in excessive reaction the attempt to try to insert liberation theology into Christian pilgrimage through encounters with Palestinian politics. It has been earnestly sustained but not very effective so far. I doubt if it will be any more successful with the average Christian visitor than lectures on the ideology of the *kibbutz* movement. If the *kibbutzim*'s image-building has been more effective, it has not been through contact with the main groups of pilgrim and tourist visitors but through the young Westerners, many Christians among them, who have taken the opportunities offered for short-term work on a *kibbutz*.

Most Christians who go to Palestine and the land of Israel have different interests and, perhaps, a sound instinct which they may find it hard to articulate into argument. The Old Testament and the Gospel which is its fulfilment do not belong to a Never-never Land of make-believe but to the history of this small country and, through it, of the world. Yet they are above and beyond the temporal history of wars and factions.

For economic and practical reasons, most modern pilgrim-tourists have gone to Israel not only on package tours but in groups, although the development of winter holidays at Eilat (and to a lesser extent beach holidays on the Mediterranean coast) may increase the proportion of independent travellers. James Currie recorded that of the 32 people on the 1958 tour led by Ronald Brownrigg mentioned in the last chapter at least 12 became group leaders taking parties to the Holy Land. The process was encouraged by the relative stability of the country after 1967 and the removal of the main visa and permit problems, but probably even more by the changes in air travel. The Vickers Viking flight to Lod in 1958 took two days and landed en route at Lyons, Brindisi, and Athens. By the 1960's that kind of journey seemed to be "hedge-hopping" compared to jet travel, even before new generations of wide-bodied aircraft trebled the capacity of a typical long-distance flight. These changes also brought down the cost of pilgrimage. That three-week tour in 1958 cost only £96, and was probably a bargain even then, but in real terms - price related to rising incomes, inflation, and other costs - the cost of packaged air and hotel travel was coming down. In 1973, for example, good-class Easter 15-day tours from Glasgow and Manchester were on offer at £143. The Great Inflation which followed both slowed down and concealed the trend (although as late as 1980 it was possible to fly by the Israeli airline El Al on a £99 off-season return), but never really reversed it.

As earlier chapters of this book have suggested, the group and package tour in various forms have usually been the pattern for Holy Land pilgrim and tourist travel. The obvious advantages have been the best possible price and, in troubled times, the best prospect of protection. Some supporters of the group tour, like James Currie, could pitch the financial argument rather strongly: "Unless you are a millionaire the only way to see the Holy Land is with a group". But he went even farther. "A highly trained British leader is essential if you are not to be exploited by guides who confuse senseless tradition with Scriptural truth." On a higher plane, however,

he suggested that in shared prayer at places like Gethsemane
or Mount Tabor: "Here the group is indispensable and the
Holy Spirit possesses his people."

That is a view worth setting against Norman Macleod's
experience in his solitary walks on the Mount of Olives or
around Nazareth, but not necessarily to be accepted. It does,
however, fit in with the movement towards more open
celebration of the Lord's Supper - or rather to reach the stage
which Protestant ecumenism had reached in Victorian Jerusalem when virtually every Presbyterian traveller from Bonar
and McCheyne onward testified to the way that the Anglicans
on Mount Zion welcomed a wide range of Christians to the
Lord's Table. Currie loved Communion on the Mount of
Olives and the Mount of Beatitudes - contrasting the situation
by the 1980s with that of his first and mainly Anglican tour in
1958. "There was a celebration of the Holy Communion
every morning which I always attended but where I was never
permitted to partake." He claimed that the outrage felt by
Anglican fellow-pilgrims at his isolation (and expressed to
Canterbury) helped to change the rules for the better.

The leader of that pioneer party, Ronald Brownrigg, set
out his own theology of pilgrimage in his handbook *Come See
the Place*, arguing that the holy sites are stage properties and
scenery in the drama of human redemption. Some tour
leaders, however, remain understandably defensive about the
"holy places" and tend to warn pilgrims in advance rather than
see them disappointed afterwards. James Martin is a Scots
minister who for many years devoted two weeks of his
holiday from a Glasgow parish to leading parties round the
Holy Land, emphasising the theme of looking for the holy
thing behind the holy place. "It is particularly necessary to
bear this in mind when we come to a site whose very
appearance may be disappointment to the first-time pilgrim"
- such as the "rather ugly building" of the Church of the Holy
Sepulchre. Apart from the contrast with the green hill far
away "there are other disappointing features like the priest
who virtually pushes the offering plate under your nose as you
stand in the little shrine of the Resurrection." The objections
and the culture-shock which the Victorians may have tended
to over-state have by no means melted away.

James Martin, writing in 1984, also took up a theme that has been relevant during most of the Holy Land's history of pilgrimage, and perhaps very similar words could have been written in Victorian times and between the two world wars.

> Many prospective Holy Land pilgrims are concerned about the political situation. Strange as it may seem, the tensions which are undoubtedly there and the problems that go with them affect the practicalities of a Holy Land pilgrimage very little. Few adjustments ever require to be made to a planned itinerary, few sites ever need to be omitted because of Israel's current relationships with her neighbours. At the same time, awareness of the tensions may well underlay a pilgrimage with a measure of sadness, and add pathos and piquancy here and there.

That remained surprisingly true even after the outbreak and sustained organisation of the *intifada* - call it uprising, unrest, or riots according to taste - in the West Bank and Gaza. There was probably less emphasis in advertising on "Hebron and Jericho, cities old before Abraham", even less inclination to go near Gaza, more wariness about Nablus. Terrorism claimed surprisingly few tourist or pilgrim victims, though many people passing through Lod airport must have vague but uneasy memories of the day when murderous Japanese fanatics, allied to Arab extremists, breached even Israel's exceptionally tight security. There was also, of course, a hidden cost in money, time, trouble and inconvenience - for example in the precautions which made it possible for El Al airline to keep flying and win a reputation for efficiency. Even the Gulf War, when Saddam Hussein's Scud missiles fell on Israel, imposed only a relatively brief interruption of the normal trends of pilgrimage and tourism.

Jewish visitors and pilgrims to Israel since 1948 have identified themselves almost totally with Israeli attitudes, though not necessarily with the opinions and actions of the Government of the day. The great majority of Christian pilgrims after 1967, like their predecessors when the land was under Muslim rule, were not primarily concerned with its politics. Many had little knowledge of them.

There were, however, two significant minorities among
Christian visitors to the Holy Land. Both had political preferences which were to be found among the expatriate Christians living in the land - ministers, priests, missionaries,
academics, teachers, students, diplomats, and a small business
and professional business community. It is impossible to
estimate either their size or any movements of opinion
statistically, and in any case numbers prove nothing. A
reasonable impression might be - though it is only an impression - that while Israel seemed in imminent danger of destruction Christian support for it was more pronounced than it was
in the 1980s, especially after the Israelis became deeply involved in the wrangles of Lebanon. There has always been a
strand of Christian Zionism in the world Church, especially
among evangelical Protestants and supporters of Jewish missions, and it survived the widespread (but not universal) move
away from missions in the traditional sense to encouragement
of Christian-Jewish relations and theological dialogue. But,
quite gradually in the 1970s and more perceptibly in the 1980s,
sympathies with the Arab predicament shaded into support
for the Palestinian cause and even, in some quarters, a tendency to incorporate an anti-Zionist outlook in theologies of
liberation.

To an extent this reflected the emphasis in these decades
on Christian involvement in politics, often expressed in
radical terms rather than conservative ones. To a limited
extent it reflected special pressures of a dubious kind, for
example in the influence of Soviet foreign policy, which was
"anti-Zionist", on East European Churches and the "Christian Peace Conference". But it also reflected the inevitable
anxieties of the Middle Eastern Churches, mainly Arab Christians in a mainly Muslim world. As Palestinians became more
frustrated and radicalised, their moods were inevitably expressed in the Churches and through the Churches.

Generalisations are misleading. Anyone who attended the
German Protestant Kirchentag in these years would be struck
by the way in which a Church with many radical tendencies
in domestic and Third World matters still tended to be very
pro-Israeli as well as pro-Jewish. German Protestants, haunted
by their country's past and the sins of other Germans, showed

much more interest than other Western Churches in relations
with the Jews and were especially sensitive to the danger that
anti-Zionism might become a cover for anti-semitism. Even
the Roman Catholic Church, though its official position
reflected a lack of enthusiasm in the Vatican for the State of
Israel, was far from monolithic. There was a powerful and
sincere lobby which saw the link between reconciliation with
the Jews and a friendlier attitude towards Israel; there were
also anti-Israeli pressures. Not till 1993 did the Vatican and
Israel agree on full diplomatic relations.

Christians in the West were influenced too by gradual
changes of attitude in their countries. In Britain there had
always been a wide range of political support for Zionism - for
example from the Cecils, Balfour, Leo Amery, and Churchill
- but there was a time when enthusiasm for the settlement of
Palestine and the emergence of Israel, with its strong elements
of Socialism, was most marked on the Left. Even as late as
1947-48 many right-wingers, including some in the British
army and the Palestinian administration, worried about the
number of Communists among Zionists. But in the years
between the Suez crisis of 1956 and the Sadat settlement a good
many Tories found an affinity with the robust nationalism
and capacity for self-defence displayed by Israel. Margaret
Thatcher was probably one of them. On the other hand it was
easier for some of those who saw world politics in terms of
haves and have-nots and development issues, and who worried
about legacies of imperialism and colonialism, to sympathise
with Arabs rather than Israelis. There were similar processes
in the United States, where Jews are traditionally liberal and
Democratic but have been inclined to become more conservative as they prosper or as they worry about law and order
issues.

One of the stranger Western Christian visitors to Israel in
1993 was the black Episcopalian mayor of New York, David
Dinkins, anxious to repair the damage done to traditional
alliances (and perhaps his own reputation) by the handling of
ethnic clashes in Brooklyn which had included black attacks
on Hasidic Jews. His entourage included 29 American Jews,
three black Baptists, two white Franciscans, a lawyer called

O'Dwyer, and an Italian-American. But he still lost his election.

Such complications, as well as the uncertainties over peace and the future of the West Bank and Gaza, point to the difficulty of predicting the future of Western relations with the powers that be, or may be, in the Holy Land. History will no more end there if there is a peace settlement than it did when the Berlin Wall came down.

But the spiritual interest in Palestine, including the Christian interest and the tradition of pilgrimage, will be one of the constant factors in a changing situation.

# 14   MEMORIES, MYSTERIES, AND CONSTANT FACTORS

## *AN EPILOGUE ON "THE PEACE OF JERUSALEM"*

Travellers, whether pilgrims or tourists or both, have always been drawn by the Holy Land, by the "desire and the dream". They have travelled in face of hazard, plague, extortion, war, and terrorism. They have seen the rise and fall of empires and the conflicts of nationalisms. Often they have travelled amid rumours of war and in the aftermath of wars. Sometimes they have been caught in wars or passed that way in the course of war. They are likely to keep on coming, whatever the political complexion of the land and however its tribes are scattered around it.

Those who reflect on their own experience, and on the experience of so many others in such different ages, will care about the future of the land and its peoples, and pray for the peace of Jerusalem.

This book first took shape amid wars and rumours of war, when Lebanon had become the most distressful country and the West Bank and Gaza were moving from sullen resentment to sustained disorder. As it goes to the publisher there are rumours of peace. Old enemies have shaken hands, though it is clear they have made new enemies among their own peoples and that there are endless opportunties for friction ahead. There are also signs of less spectacular but practical co-operation. It is possible again to see Jordanian tourism trying to attract Western visitors, and offering Amman airport as a starting point for tours taking in Petra as well as the Holy Land.

Attempting to predict the future is a dangerous business, especially in a region as unstable as the Middle East has been since the downfall of the Ottoman Empire and the end of the brief interlude of British domination. Yet there are some factors so constant and aspirations so powerful that it is reasonable to expect them to influence the course of affairs. How they interact will determine whether harmonies or discords are to be most audible in these Middle Eastern themes. Among the constant factors are these:

- The Christian interest in the land of Christ.

- The ancient and modern attachment of the people of Israel, whether as citizens of the Jewish State or Jews of the dispersion, to the land of Israel.

- The paradox that Arab nationalism is expressed both in the aspiration for a sense of greater Arab nationality and in tenacious attachment to the existing and more local Arab identities, including now a Palestinian one.

- The special role of Arab culture, language, and history in the worldwide religion of Islam, in a situation where the great majority of Muslims are not Arabs and substantial Arab minorities are not Muslims.

- The role of the land as a meeting-place of Western and Eastern Christianity.

- The historic uncertainty whether Palestine is to be a meeting-place or a battle-ground between the West and East.

I end this book by looking at each of these constant factors in turn.

So long as the Gospel is preached and the Gospels are read, Christians will interest themselves in the land of Jesus. I offer that as a low-key statement in terms from which the apathetic and indifferent, as well as the atheist and agnostic, would find it hard to dissent. Christians can go much farther, given what they believe about who was born in Bethlehem, crucified in Jerusalem, and encountered again elsewhere, whether on the road to Emmaus or by the lakeside in Galilee. It is a thing most wonderful that the things "almost too wonderful to be" should relate so definitely to particular places as well as a particular time, even though for nearly 2000 years they have been universally available across all boundaries of geography and nationality.

For some the visit to the places of these memories and mysteries will still be the desire and dream of a lifetime, as well as a time to distinguish between the essentials and the mere trappings of Christianity. As Bernard Fergusson wrote - echoing in a gentler modern mood the culture-shock which the Protestant Victorians felt so acutely - "they may not even care for all they see at the so-called holy places, though the devotion of centuries about them count for something."

But it is unimportant whether individual locations can be identified or not - even the location of Calvary and the tomb - and it is a matter of personal inclination as well as opportunity whether Christians visit the Holy Land or not. They will encounter no real presence there that is not accessible elsewhere and, however pious and extensive their travels, they will win no favour here or for eternity except through Grace.

However, those remembered in this book indicate the range of Christians setting out on the road to Zion and the reflections stirred in them by the Holy Land. The appearance of the land and the customs of its people have changed and are likely to go on changing. The nature of the Christian experience in it will not change.

. And that Christian experience cannot be separated from that Jewish attachment of the people of Israel to the land of Israel. It is not only that Jesus was a Jew, but that the Old Testament which was his Bible must always be an integral part of Christian history, theology, and spiritual experience. Israel is not only a State in the land, nor even just a strange and wonderful people. It is also a mystery... a mystery from which emerge indications of God's purposes not just for one people but for all peoples.

That does not mean that there is not something wonderful in the restoration of the State of Israel in the Holy Land, despite all the conflict and at times cruelty of the long Jewish-Arab conflict. By all human standards the sequence of events has led to an astonishing achievement based on a series of extreme improbabilities. And those who think that human standards are not everything cannot be unmoved by the apparent fulfilment of biblical prophecies, however dimly we understand them or rashly interpret them. We may have doubts about how precisely modern events relate to Ezekiel's

vision (36.33-36) of replanting desolation, resettling towns,
and rebuilding ruins; or Amos's vision (9.11) of restoring
David's fallen tent or tabernacle; or to Isaiah's image (60.11) of
the ever-open gates; or to Zecharaiah's vision (8.3 and 12.3) of
Jerusalem as immovable rock for all the nations and city of
truth. But they must be reverent doubts, in the context of the
fulfilment of God's promises Christians find in Jesus.

Even on the most practical level, the Jewish attachment to
the land of Israel must be taken into account in Christian-
Jewish relations. It is true that anti-Zionism is not the same
thing as anti-semitism, though it was not only in Soviet Russia
that the one could overlap with the other. Christians may
argue that the Balfour Declaration was a mistake, even con-
ceivably that modern political Zionism is a distortion of the
hope of return that pre-Zionist Jews shared with Victorian
Christians like Shaftesbury, Bonar, and McCheyne. They
may also hold that much injustice has been suffered by many
Arabs, both before and after the creation of the State of Israel.

But all these arguments can no longer be urged as if the
Holocaust had never happened, even though those responsible were essentially anti-Christian as well as anti-Jewish: and
as if the State of Israel had not had to fight so long and hard for
its independence and its survival. Whatever God's ultimate
purposes for the Jewish people - "beloved for their fathers'
sake" - the basis of Christian-Jewish relations must include
acceptance of the State of Israel in the Land of Israel and
recognition of the ties which bind to it even those Jews who
have no thought of emigrating or giving up their British or
American nationality and citizenship. That does not mean
supporting the actions of particular Governments of Israel,
any more than all Israelis feel they have to support them. It
does mean recognition that the national home must survive as
a nation-State.

But what of the national home for the Arabs whom even
the Israelis now call Palestinians? In 1917 there was no
Palestinian nation, not even a Turkish province of Palestine,
but people are what they feel themselves to be and what
circumstances make them. There is now a sense of Palestinian
identity which in some ways may be stronger than any sense
of Lebanese, Iraki, or even Syrian identity. Those who share

it are not only in the "occupied territories" of the West Bank and Gaza - including the areas specified for self-government in the 1993 accord - but in other Arab countries and within Israel. This book is not the place to speculate about the political format within which that sense of nationality could be expressed, or the relationship that Arabs on one bank of the Jordan can have with those on the other.

Neither the West nor the Israelis can dictate. They have to wait and see, and keep open minds. They also have to accept the paradox that the Arabs will try to express their cultural unity and common identity amid many Arab rivalries and quarrels. That should not altogether surprise Europeans, whose own civilisation for centuries expressed a similar paradox.

It is important to realise that Arab and Muslim are not quite the same thing, though the role of Arabs in the foundation and expansion of Islam, and of Arabic in its faith and culture, will always make it difficult to keep the concepts entirely separate. The future of Islam is likely to be much influenced by developments in Pakistan, Central Asia, Indonesia, and Africa. But even the rise of Muslim "fundamentalism" is by no means mainly an Arab phenomenon. It is to be found in such Muslim peoples as the Turks and not just among Libyans or the Egyptian and Algerian oppositions; and its most spectacular assertion in world affairs has come from the non-Arab Shia Muslims of Iran, one of whose achievements has been to revive and radicalise the hitherto neglected Arab Shias in Lebanon. There are also parts of the Islamic world where civil wars, for example involving Iraki or Turkish Kurds, will rouse more enthusiasm than holy wars.

But one of the urgent reasons for the West to work for an Israeli-Arab settlement is the danger that the political issues will become entangled with an apparent confrontation of religions. If the quarrel continues, the Arabs will inevitably play the Islamic card in propaganda aimed to win moral or financial support from the Muslim world. They will also, in their appeal to the West, quite correctly remind it of the presence of the Christian Arab minority among the Palestinians and in Israel, where it has the problems of being a minority in a minority. The West raised both the hopes and the status of the Arab Christians during the decline and fall of the oppressive Ottoman Empire, but subsequent events have tended to depress them again. The Palestinian Arab Christians have suffered more than their share of tribulations and many of their educated, able, ambitious, and moderate people have emigrated.

The West needs to remind itself that there are not only two nationalities in the Holy Land but a wider range of communities, including the Christian ones. It should also encourage its cultural links with the Christians of Lebanon and rediscover its affinities with the other Christian minorities of the Arab and the wider Islamic world, including the large Coptic minority of Egypt and the ancient Churches in Syria and Irak.

The Holy Land has in its long history been both a meeting-place and a battle-ground. It has maintained that tradition in the years since the restoration of Israel as a State. For vast numbers of Westerners it has been their only glimpse of Asia, a kind of extended day-trip into another civilisation. For many Western Christians, Protestants and Roman Catholic alike, it has provided their main encounter with Eastern Christianity.

How long the land remains a battle-ground depends primarily on the accommodation of the long-festering Arab-Israeli quarrel. It seems naive to expect that to happen quickly or smoothly, whatever happens in Jericho and Gaza, between Israel and Jordan, and within Jordan. The complexity of Palestinian politics, the fanaticism or instability within various Arab States, the situation of Jerusalem, the Jewish settlements beyond pre-1967 Israel, the probable growth of Israel's Arab minority, and the uncertainties of coalition and longterm opinion in Israel: all these make it rash to predict a peaceful future. But the settlement with Egypt and the progress with the Palestinians were not easily come by either. It is a time to hope and pray.

Whatever the course of the quarrels and the attempts at settlement the Holy Land will remain a meeting-place. Israel will not only be a factor in the West's Christian-Jewish relations, but will change their context even when it adds to their complexity. In one country an anxious, sensitive, easily alarmed minority will be the Christian and not a Jewish one.

The complexities of the Jews as a nation, of Israel as a State, and of Judaism as a religion will (as already happens) bring perplexities for the Jewish judges and politicians in Israel. There will be "Messianic Jews" and other Jewish Christians who do not (as usually happens in the West) become an enrichment of the Gentile communities but will testify among their own people where their home is.

When Christians think of Jews it will neither be of a despised, depressed and distrusted minority (as often happened in the past) nor of talented, gifted, and prosperous minorities, as often happens today; rather it will be of a people who have everywhere, but most obviously in Israel, the diversities which are found within the unity of any nation, as well as a unique history and place in history. It is less clear what kind of meeting-place the Holy Land and its surroundings will be for Christianity and Islam. For this is where Islam (like medieval Christianity) has never shown itself to best advantage. Save for the Haram built on the foundations of the Temple, with the great Dome of the Rock and some lesser buildings of grace and beauty, it has surprisingly few Islamic monuments of importance. The last centuries of Muslim Government left a memory of inefficiency, cruelty, extortion, and tyranny. They left no artistic, philosophical, and scientific afterglow of achievement like that of Moorish Spain, the most tolerant and human face of Islam. For though Jerusalem was a place of Arab holiness and Muslim pilgrimage it was not a place of activity and achievement like Damascus and Baghdad. The future dialogues of Christianity and Islam will probably be based and inspired elsewhere.

Yet if peace could come to the Holy Land it would encourage all kinds of personal and cultural contacts in which Western Christians would encounter local Christians as well as Jews and Muslims. As I write I have remembered just in time to support a fellow-elder who is ready to pedal on a "biblical bike ride" from Nazareth to Bethlehem in aid of the Edinburgh Medical Missionary Society's hospital. The Holy Land is a very special country but in modern conditions it need not seem a very distant one. Nor, if peace could break out and be given a chance, need it seem a terribly strange one.

What of the Holy Land as a meeting-place of Christians of different ideas, backgrounds, and traditions? As the earlier chapters of this book have shown, it has always had such a role to some extent. Protestants and Roman Catholics still found some cultural affinity even in times of their most acute political and theological confrontations, Westerners in an Eastern land. But both, in face of Muslim preponderance and Turkish power, crossed some of the cultural barriers separating them from the Eastern Orthodox Churches.

That wonderful but not always dependable travel classic from the 1830's, A.W. Kinglake's *Eothen*, has among its best passages one about an encounter in Damascus with a Syrian Christian who rejoiced in the way Westerners insisted on using the walkway above the bridle-road, once called "the path of the faithful" and denied to Jews and native Christians. Kinglake derided a tendency to look down on Oriental Christians as "dissenters from the established religion of a Mahometan empire" and "felt the more strongly for my creed when I saw it despised among men.... I heard, as I fancied, the faint echo of an old crusader's conscience that whispered and said: Common Cause."

The common cause cannot be forgotten, though it is not served by political lobbying, whether against the old Muslim ascendancy or the new Jewish one in Israel.

There are those who still wonder what the role of the Holy Land might be if and when Christendom finds that the universal Church has established a visible unity. If it ever needs a patriarch and permanent moderator for its grandest synod - which I doubt - the most appropriate place is probably not Rome, nor Geneva nor Constantinople, but Jerusalem.

> We still experience a sort of patriotism for Palestine and feel that the scenes enacted there were performed for the whole family of man. Narrow as are its boundaries we have all a share in the possession: what a church is to a city, Palestine is to the world.

So wrote the Anglican traveller Eliot Warburton in 1847, but the substance of the thought has survived the many political changes since.

Provided the Holy City is never forced to relocate the bureaucracies of Rome and the World Council of Churches - their accommodation would surely stretch all the way down to Jericho - Jerusalem is the most obvious and impartial choice to be the titular capital of a confederation of the visible Church. It could from time to time have some such symbolic and ceremonial role without predudice to its secular role as capital of the State of Israel or its supreme spiritual importance in the Jewish religion and its important place in the Muslim one.

Meanwhile it is best to pray for the peace of Jerusalem, and to recognise that the prayer may bear a double meaning. It is a prayer for the unity and amity of the household of faith, for all those who seek citizenship of the city of God. It is also a prayer for the peoples of the city and of the land whose history and experiences, and whose place in God's scheme of revelation and reconciliation, make it holy, even though it must never become (in the cautionary phrase of Eliot Warburton) a "geographical object of idolatry".

In the words of the Scots metrical form of Psalm 122:
Pray that Jerusalem may have
Peace and felicity;
Let them that love thee and thy peace
Have still prosperity.

We wish peace within her walls, and in the land around, for what the Psalmist calls our "companions' sakes". And all who give thanks to the name of the Lord are our companions.

But remember Norman Macleod's thoughts from the Mount of Olives. Simple faith and childlike love bring access everywhere and not just in a chosen land to "the presence, the grace, and the peace of Christ... Most thankful was I for knowing that the person, not the place, was holy - that his love was not local but universal."

# APPENDIX:

# NOTES ON BOOKS AND SOURCES

These chapter-by-chapter notes indicate sources, identify the more important quotations, and provide a selective bibliography. Anyone who reads and researches on Holy Land matters will soon acquire a new sense of what being selective means. It is impossible to read everything and difficult enough to remember what one has read!

## CHAPTER 1: THE DESIRE AND THE DREAM

For my summary of pre-Victorian travels to Palestine, including Arculf, Saewulf, Willibald, and Maundrell I found the collection of *Early Travels to Palestine* in Bohn's Antiquarian Library (London, 1848) most convenient. This also contains versions of the notable Jewish traveller and rabbi Benjamin of Tudela, and of "Sir John Maundeville", who is easily found separately. For the argument questioning Maundeville's authenticity see *Medieval Travellers* by Margaret Wade Labarge (London 1982) which is good about pilgrimage and a helpful guide to source material.

There is a vast literature on the Crusades, with Lord Runciman's *History of the Crusades* (London, from 1950) the great modern work. I found useful the East German Martin Erbtösser's *The Crusades* (English translation Newton Abbot, 1978).

The easiest access to Richard Hakluyt is probably the Everyman edition. I found Aldersey among other Levant travels in Volume 3.

There is a good modern *Life and Adventures of Thomas Coryate* by Michael Strachan (Oxford 1962) with some notes about Lithgow based on the 1760 Edinburgh edition of his *Travels*. This also notes the travels of Moryson and Sandys. For the troubles of Thomas Shaw see his *Travels in Barbary and the Levant* (London 1738). Chateaubriand's *Itinéraire de Paris à Jérusalem* is in a modern Garnier Flammarion paperback (Paris 1968).

The quotation from Michael Russell is from *Palestine or the Holy Land* (Edinburgh, 1832) a book which shows the attention

given to Bonaparte's curious proclamation. Robert Curzon's
1849 *Visits to the Monasteries of the Levant* with the account of the
Holy Fire disaster has recently been republished (London 1983).

For a general view of the history of pilgrimage there is
*Pilgrims to the Holy Land* by Teddy Kollek and Moshe Pearlman.
This is better on the Jewish tradition than the Christian one but
useful.

## CHAPTER 2: THE SCOTS RECONNAISSANCE

I do not not know of any modern edition of Bonar and McCheyne's
*Narrative of a Mission of Enquiry to the Jews* (Edinburgh 1842 and
subsequent editions or printings) though I understand that a
major scholarly work on it is in prospect. There are modern
editions of Bonar's life of McCheyne and of McCheyne's ser-
mons. The story of the 1839 expedition and its aftermath is told
in David McDougall's "Chronicle of the Jewish missions of the
Church of Scotland" *In Search of Israel* (London 1940).

Sir Moses Montefiore's diaries were published (London
1890).Books about him include those by Lucien Wolf (London
1884) and Paul Goodman (Philadelphia 1925).

The Irish Presbyterian Missionary Herald from 1841 onwards carried remarkable evidence of the impact of Bonar and
McCheyne on Irish missions. There are some graphic and at
times harrowing descriptions of the conflicts which have become
familiar to us through the troubles of modern Lebabon - notably
by William Graham in 1843. But I reluctantly decided that this
book could not deal except in passing with Syria and Lebanon.

I took the McCheyne poem from Bonar's book *Palestine for
the Young* (London c.1855) though it may appear elsewhere.

## CHAPTER 3: THE VIENNESE LADY, THE ARTIST, AND
## THE HEBREW BISHOP

Ida Pfeiffer's travel books had a vogue at the time in English
translation as well as German, as references by other Victorian
travellers make clear, and deserve to benefit from the current
feminist vogue in publishing. However I have used the only
modern version of Reise einer Wienerin in das heilige Land
(Stuttgart 1968) which I have encountered.

W.H. Bartlett's *Walks around Jerusalem* (London 1844) and
*Jerusalem Revisited* (London 1855) have both been reprinted in
facsimile in modern Israel. The former has a useful introduction
by Rechavam Zeevy which includes a reference to recent Hebrew
work on Victorian Christian travellers. For Thackeray see Notes
Ch.7.

There is a modern republication of David Roberts' pictures
and diary *The Holy Land* (British edition, 1982). The definitive
work on Scottish artists, including Wilkie, is Duncan Macmillan's
*Scottish Art 1460-1990* (Edinburgh 1990).

I found Barbara Tuchman's *Bible and Sword* (New York,
1956) useful on British attitudes to the Holy Land. It covers the
bishopric and much else. It is a work of distinction spoiled by a
lack of sympathy with Evangelical (and other) Christianity so
great that it also involves a lack of understanding. Any biography
of Shaftesbury is a useful corrective. Tuchman has, however, an
admirable bibliography up to her time. There is a valuable
account of the Jerusalem bishopric plan and controversy in
Volume 1 of the WCC *History of the Ecumenical Movement*
(Geneva edition 1986) but it is characteristic of our time that the
Jewish mission aspect is hardly mentioned.

## CHAPTER 4: QUEEN VICTORIA'S MAN GOES EAST

I have never encountered Norman Macleod's *Eastward* in its
book form but used the original serialised version in the 1865
*Good Words*.

Edward Jonas's *Recollections of Syria and Palestine* (London,
1857) deals with the country some years before its publication.
Disraeli is quoted from the life by R.W. Davis (London 1876).
There is a full account of *Disraeli's Grand Tour* by Robert Blake
(London 1982).

J. Ivor Murray's unpublished account of of his visit to
Jerusalem, including the Haram, and to other parts of Palestine
is in the National Library of Scotland (Ms 9843). Among other
curiosities it contains an analysis of the nationality of pilgrims
staying at the Franciscan hospice in Nazareth 1850-54. The
largest identifiable group of about 20 per cent was English
(presumably including other British, but with one Australian
noted separately) followed by French, Italians, and Americans.

Also in the National Library of Scotland is an exercise book containing the letters to his mother of one of Norman Macleod's travelling companions, William Mure of Caldwell (Ms. 2733). I am grateful to the Trustees of the Library for permission to quote from this and other collections mentioned.

Fergus Ferguson, the Prince-of-Wales-watcher in *Sacred Scenes in Egypt and the Holy Land* (Glasgow 1864) is not to be confused with the James Fergusson, a notable architectural writer, who had a brief vogue after 1847 with a theory that the real Holy Sepulchre was on the Temple Mount. Another Victorian sepulchre theory was that of Colonel Conder (Palestine Exploration Fund Quarterly 1881).

## CHAPTER 5: ECCENTRICS, SOLDIERS, AND SURVEYS

Rebecca West's account of Jeanne Merkus appears in *Black Lamb and Grey Falcon* (pp. 271-3, one-volume edition, London 1955) and Bertha Spafford Vester's in *Our Jerusalem*, an untidy but immensely valuable book of memories covering nearly 60 years (British edition, London 1951). Mrs Vester writes about almost everyone who was anyone in Jerusalem, including General Gordon, whose Calvary theories are dealt with fairly by his modern biographer, Charles Chenevix Trench. Barbara Tuchman (see Ch.3 notes) is better on the soldiers and surveyors than on the missionaries.

I used a privately supplied photocopy of the Wilson Ordnance map of Jerusalem. Martin Gilbert's 1977 *Jerusalem Illustrated History Atlas* (British, American, and Israeli editions) is valuable for this era, as well as for earlier and later ones, not least for rational estimates of Jerusalem's population. The description of Warren and his men at work is from *In the Holy Land* by Andrew Thomson (London 1874). Thomson's account of landing at Jaffa contains my favourite phrase about the "desire and the dream of a lifetime".

Thomson is not to be confused with the American W.M. Thomson, whose *The Land and the Book* had a prodigious sale and influence. It exists in several versions and revisions. I used the 1877 London one-volume edition and the two London volumes of 1881-83.

Henry Rider Haggard's view of the Garden Tomb is in *A Winter Pilgrimage* (London, 1904). Dr James Robertson's ap-

in the 1892 Life and Work in which he wrote four articles about
a Holy Land visit. I hoped to find in them some enthusiasm for
Jewish settlement which might have influenced his parishioner
Balfour but the references to modern Jews are rather conventional
descriptions of Wailing Wall scenes. However, the congregation
at Whittingehame must have heard a lot about Old Testament
geography and history!

Arthur Stanley's *Sinai and Palestine* appeared in 1856 but was
later updated. I used the "new edition" (London 1887).

John MacGregor's inland voyage appeared as *The Rob Roy on
the Jordan* (London 1869). H.B. Tristram's journal appeared as
*The Land of Israel* (London 1865). Agnes Smith's *Eastern Pilgrims*
apeared under her maiden name (London 1870). There is an
account of her scholarship, marriage to Samuel Lewis, and work
with her sister in *The Ladies of Castlebrae* by A. Whigham Price
(Gloucester 1985).

George Pitt's story was narrated in *The British Friend* in 1882
and reprinted in *Remarkable Travels* (Glasgow, 1886). The cruise
prices quoted are from the Lunn-Perowne cruise advertisements
of 1896.

## CHAPTER 6: THE SCRAMBLE FOR PALESTINE

A most valuable book, for itself and as a guide to other works, is
*The Zionist Movement in Palestine and World Politics 1880-1918*
edited by N. Gordon Levin (Lexington, Mass. 1974). Chaim
Weizmann's autobiography *Trial and Error* (London 1949) is
important for the whole second half of this book. There is a vast
bibliography on Herzl and on Zionism (which has an encyclo-
paedia).

The quarterly transactions of the Palestine Exploration Fund
are immensely valuable. I have quoted Wilson and others from
the 1899 annual meeting. The P.E.F. also has much information
about the Kaiser's Palestinian visit of 1898. George Adam Smith's
*The Historical Geography of the Holy Land* (London 1894 and
many subsequent editions) is one of the great books about
Palestine. I discussed it in private conversations with his son, the
late Lord Balerno. His daughter, Dr Janet Adam Smith, very
kindly arranged for me to have access to her father's papers in the
National Library of Scotland when they were still private property. They have since passed into the Library's ownership (Acc.

9446) and I am grateful to Dr Adam Smith and the Trustees of the Library for permission to quote from them.

Smith's family connections also included a nephew who made his mark in public life: R.A. Butler, probably the most influential Conservative this century to be denied tenancy of 10 Downing Street.

Robert Black's notes of his journey in 1895 are in the National Library of Scotland: Acc. 7953 (ii).

I inspected the vistors' book at Tabeetha School in Jaffa during one of my visits there and found a wealth of distinguished signatories, including a number of those mentioned in this book, among them John MacGregor (at rest from his canoeing), George Adam Smith on his first visit to Palestine, Archbishop Randall Davidson etc. The late Isobel Goodwin assisted me with information about Jane Walker Arnott. The 1879 first volume of Life and Work has an an account of the school by Jane's sister Emily who later handled the fund-raising at home.

Elizabeth Butler's Palestinian pictures are in her *Letters from the Holy Land* (London 1903).

There is a good introduction to Arab nationalism in Peter Mansfield's *The Arabs* (London 1976). A classic Arab view written before the great Middle East troubles is *The Arab Awakening* by George Antonius (Phildelphia 1939). The Revd Frederick Levison drew my atention to recollections of his Uncle Nahum in which I found the contrast between calm in Safed and Arab-Jewish friction in Jerusalem before the end of the century.

Dr David Torrance told the Scots United Free Church Record of the Tiberias rejoicing over the 1908 Turkish revolution. He gave an account, from a more distant perspective, to his biographer W.P. Livingstone for *A Galilee Doctor* (London 1923).

The 1888 estimated population figure for Syria and Palestine is taken from the 1895 edition of Longmans' Gazeteer of the World.

## Chapter 7: The Russian Connection

By far the most important book is Stephen Graham's *With the Russian Pilgrims to Jerusalem* (London 1913).

There is correspondence about Russian travellers in the Smith papers. The curious items about the chariot-wheels and the burning bush I found in E.S. Bates' *Touring in 1600* (London 1911, also 1987 edition). Tristram's book and Agnes Smith's are noted for Ch.5, Macleod's for Ch.4. Eliot Warburton's encounter at Mar Saba is from *The Crescent and the Cross*. It sold well. My 1859 edition (16 years after the events it describes) is the fifteenth. W.M. Thackeray's *Cornhill to Cairo* (London 1846) is most easily found in collected editions of his works.

Charles Dudley Warner's observation is from *In the Levant* (1876). It also sold well. My edition is the sixteenth (Boston 1889). The story of the attempted theft from the party of Wallace Brown is from a reprint (Inverness 1896) of *Letters from Sunny Shores* to a local newspaper. Pierre Loti's encounter is from *Jérusalem* (Paris 1895). Harold Copping's meeting with the procession comes from *A Journalist in the Holy Land* (London 1913), coinciding with Robert Hichens' *The Holy Land*. Wilson's comments are in his address to the 1899 P.E.F. annual meeting, published with its quarterly statement.

The reference to the brief post-war revival of Russian pilgrimage is from *Paterson of Hebron* by W. Ewing (London 1930). The point about the late Archbishop Nikodim is made from personal observation of him at several meetings of the Central Committee of the World Council of Churches (which I attended as a journalist).

A English translation of the book *Joseph Rabinowitz* by the Danish writer Kai Kjaer-Hansen will be published in 1994 by the Handsel Press and Eerdmans.

## CHAPTER 8: WAR CHANGES EVERYTHING

Livingstone (Notes Ch.6) and Mrs Vester (Notes Ch.5) are useful for the outbreak of war. For the main campaign I made much use of the *52nd Lowland Division 1914-18* by R.R. Thompson (Glasgow, 1923). There are vivid accounts of the Judean hill fighting by an unnamed chaplain in Life and Work for 1918. Liddell Hart's views on the Palestinian campaign are found in his *History of the World War 1914-18* (London 1934). T.E. Lawrence's veiled eagerness to be at the Allenby entry to Jerusalem is found in the *Seven Pillars of Wisdom* (p.462 Penguin edition). Clement Hankey's walking tour is described in *Walks in the Holy Land 1918-19* (London 1920).

Robert Wilson's letters and commentaries on *Palestine 1917* were published after his death (Tunbridge Wells 1987). The title is misleading, as there is interesting material from 1916 in Sinai and the 1918 advance far into Syria.

The vivid memories of Joseph Baratz are in *A Village by the Jordan* (Tel Aviv 1960 edition). The advice about the Bible as guide book is noted by Edward Thompson (see Ch.10 notes).

The McBey picture was on exhibition at the Royal Scottish Academy during the 1993 Edinburgh festival.

## CHAPTER 9: A DECLARATION OF AMBIGUITY

The material about Sir George Adam Smith is taken from his papers in the National Library of Scotland (see Ch.6 notes) though the pamphlet referred to there (London 1918) was widely circulated.

There is a vast bibliography on the Balfour Declaration and much on Balfour himself. It all leaves open some of the questions I have tried to discuss, if not exactly answer. Weizmann is vital reading, but one still asks afterwards: "How did he manage it?"

The Lloyd George memoirs and biographies are tediously unrevealing but there is insight in the brief coverage in John Marlowe's *Milner: Apostle of Empire* (London 1976).

For the baptismal names of Andrew Bonar Law see Robert Blake's *The Unknown Prime Minister* (London 1955). His mother really wanted to call him after McCheyne but already had a Robert. Bonar Law was not one of the British politicians especially involved with Zionism.

## CHAPTER 10: BRITAIN'S THANKLESS MANDATE

The Edward Thompson quotation is from *Crusader's Coast* (London 1929). Sir Ronald Storrs' apologia is in *Orientations* (London 1937).

I used the 1924 edition of the Thomas Cook *Traveller's Handbook for Palestine and Syria* and the 1923 London edition of Father Barnabas Meistermann's *Guide to the Holy Land*.

For this and the two subsequent chapters I was often guided by a very fine history, *Cross-roads to Israel* by Christopher Sykes (London 1965). For Paterson see Ch.7 notes, for David Torrance Ch.6, for Bernard Fergusson Ch. 11. Winston Churchill's activities are well described by Martin Gilbert in Volume Four of the official biography (London 1975). Hansard gives the full text of speeches to the House of Commons. Herbert Torrance's comment on Tiberias in 1929 is from his report to the Scottish Church (whose reunion turned his hospital that year from a United Free to a C. of S. one).

I am indebted to the Very Revd Professor T.F.Torrance for information about his time in the Middle East, including Palestine, Irak, and Syria in 1936 shortly after the outbreak of the Arab Rebellion. It comes from conversations and from a private memoir of his travels which he let me have.

## CHAPTER 11: AN APPROACHING DISASTER

Sykes' history is a good guide to the mass of official and parliamentary reports, as well as to the development of the tragedy. His *Orde Wingate* (London 1959) is also necessary reading.

Maurice Pearlman's adventures and opinion are in *Collective Adventure* (London 1938). J.W. Clapham's *Palestine, the Land of my Adoption* appeared during the Second World War but its conversations seem to date from an earlier time. The hopes of the Hebrew Christians and the role of Sir Leon Levison are major themes of *Christian and Jew: Leon Levison* by Frederick Levison (Edinburgh1989).

St John Ervine's *A Journey to Jerusalem* (London 1936) is vinegary and H. V. Morton's *In the Steps of the Master* (London 1934) a bit sugary.

The wartime sojourn of John Connell was in *The House by Herod's Gate* (London 1946), source of the quotation about the thump and lift of the heart, and Steven (Lord) Runciman's essay into radio newsreading is described in *A Traveller's Alphabet* (London 1991). Bernard Fergusson's account of his flight over the troubled land comes from *The Trumpet in the Hall* (London 1970) which has much insight from a fair-minded man, fine soldier, and good Christian caught in a hopeless situation.

Clark Kerr's messages and John Fraser's account of the moderatorial visit in the last weeks of the Mandate are quoted from Life and Work issues of 1948. Mrs Frances Macnab kindly gave me access to private notes, papers, and cuttings (notably from the Aberdeen Press and Journal) about this visit by her

father, the Very Revd Dr Matthew Stewart. Aspects of the
fighting are well handled from a soldiers's viewpoint in Sir John
Glubb's *A Soldier with the Arabs* (London 1957) and from a
journalistic one in the pro-Jewish *O Jerusalem* by Larry Colline
and Dominique Lapierre (London 1972). Its bibliography is a
useful summary of the mass of argument, history, and memoir.

## CHAPTER 12: ISRAEL RESTORED: THE LAND DIVIDED

Sykes is as fair as anyone can be about the independence of Israel
as well as the Mandate. There are translated memoirs from many
of the Israeli politicians involved. Weizmann remains valuable.

The quotations from Zev Vilnay's *The Guide to Israel* are
from the eighth edition (Jerusalem 1965). Ethel Mannin's views
are in *The Lovely Land* (London 1965). Betty Hartman Wolf's
warning about Jordanian demands for evidence of Church membership is on p.261 of *Journey through the Holy Land* (New York
1967).

Terence Prittie's *Israel: Miracle in the Desert* (New York 1967)
is a cut above most of the hymns of praise for Israel. It also catches
the mood of the years just before the Six Day War. Mansfield's
book (see Ch.6 notes) is useful.

## CHAPTER 13: PILGRIMS AND TOURISTS

James Currie and James Martin are quoted from articles I
commissioned for Life and Work (January 1984). Martin has also
the helpful *A Plain Man in the Holy Land* (Edinburgh 1978).
Ronald Brownrigg's classic handbook is *Come See the Place*
(London 1985).

Mayor Dinkins' curious but unrewarding pilgrimage was
described at length in The New Yorker of August 2, 1993.

## CHAPTER 14: MEMORIES, MYSTERIES, AND
## CONSTANT FACTORS

Canon Brownrigg, James Martin, and Jerome Murphy-O'Connor
in his archaeological guide *The Holy Land* (Oxford 1980) cover a
wide range of approaches to "holy places".

*Palestine Comes First* by the Dutch Dominican Lucas
Grollenberg (English translation London 1980) is the clearest

exposition of the move of some left-wing Christians towards a strongly pro-Palestinian position. It has a useful bibliography. A similar but secular approach comes in Gerard Chaliand's *The Palestinian Resistance* (Penguin translation 1972).

Arab accounts of the situation include Ibrahim Al-Abid's *PLO Handbook to the Palestinian Question* (Beirut 1969) and *Bitter Harvest: Palestine 1914-67* by Sami Hadawi (New York 1967).

From the vast Jewish literature on Israel, self-critical or uncritical, I mention Ronald Segal's *Whose Israel?* (London 1972), despite disproportionate interest in Socialist aspects of Zionism. *The Rebirth and Restoration of Israel* by Murray Dixon (Chichester 1988) is a popular evangelical Christian Zionist approach, very pro-Jewish and more theological than political. There are deeper theological reflections related to Israel - as people, State, and theological concept - in *The Witness of the Jews to God* edited by D.W. Torrance (Edinburgh 1982), with important essays by T.F. Torrance and J.K.S. Reid. A short introduction to the meanings of "Israel" is Jock's Stein's article in the April 1983 Life and Work. Samuel Hosain's Handsel Press pamphlet *Israel Reassessed* (Edinburgh 1988) comes from an unusual pro-Arab viewpoint, the author being a Christian minister of North African Muslim origin.

The prospect of peace will bring a new wave of contemporary books about Israel and her neighbours. A reasonably detached view is from the broadcaster Gerald Butt, whose analysis of Israel *Behind the Star* (London 1990) was preceded by his *The Arab World*.

The Bernard Fergusson (Lord Ballantrae) quotation is from the last piece he wrote, a commemoration of the St Andrew's Jerusalem jubilee for Life and Work in November 1980. He died before the commemorative service, at which his seat of honour stayed vacant.

A.W. Kinglake's curious but moving dissertation on the despised Christians under Turkish rule will be found on pp 222-3 of the Everyman edition of *Eothen*.

# INDEX